PREFACE

Language aims at communication. Effective communication is a skill; if learnt assidously, it can add to one's status. Composition both free and guided helps to develop this art. Effective communication enriches our life and helps to achieve rapport between man and society. Better communication requires a strong foot board of comprehention. Essay writing is an interesting tool of self expression. Textual information is today given secondary importance. Such topics are set in examination which reveal that besides bookish knowledge what other relevant and though provoking material they have gathered from the world. It is thus the harmonious blending of `thought' and `expression'. The one without the other makes it defective. If thoughts are wanting essay becomes verbose, if language does not properly express the thought, it becomes clumsy and unreal.

—**Author**

Modern School Essays, Letters & Short Stories

A complete Book of School Essays, Letters & Short Stories

H.C. Gulati

M.A. (Eng.), M.Ed.

Central School, Salt Lake, Kolkata

MINI BOOKS
PUBLISHERS

MODERN SCHOOL ESSAYS,
LETTERS & SHORT STORIES

Revised Edition : 2011

Price : ₹ 60.00 only

Published by :
MINI BOOKS
(An Imprint of Chaudhary Book Company)
Lal Kurti, Meerut -- 250 001 (INDIA)
Ph. : Off. (0121) -- 2645252
e-mail : minibooks.publishers@gmail.com

Laser Typesetting :
Sunbeam Computers, Meerut

Printed at :
J.C.T. Offset, Meerut

CONTENT

ESSAYS

LETTER-WRITING

MODEL LETTERS

LETTERS

SHORT STORIES

ESSAY WRITING

INTRODUCTION

An essay is a short composition on any subject. It should have elegant style. A natural and easy narration obviously fits in to this. According to Benson, "The essential point about an essay is not the subject but charm it exudes".

The essay has been variously classified but it must be own on mind that this classification is only a theoretical propensity. Infact any given essay indifferent part is found to include all to the zoo may be descriptive in name but he emotional and aesthetic glow of writers personality shall definitely colour its web.

According to the subject matter and form, essay can be divided as under :

(1) **Descriptive Essays.** These are those that consists of description of some place or thing. They require exact knowledge of place or object, its salient features. The description should be both clear and pleasant. The writer of the description should set to work in the manner of a painter vivid and graphic.

(2) **Narrative Essays.** The subject matter of narrative essay is the same as that of narrative proper. It consists of the narration of some event, action or movement. The event may be imaginary or historical or a personal experience of student.

This form of essay is written in the form of a story. The student may be asked to write about the biographical sketch of well-known persons, a journey or a voyage or an accident like a street quarrel or a bus accident. The setting and atmosphere is necessary as it grants colour, life, movement and fullness to the emotional glow of the narrative.

(3) **Reflective Essays.** In a descriptive essay, the student writes what he has seen, what he has done himself or seen or heard other people doing, but in the reflective essay, he is required to record what he has thought. The aim of reflective essay is to test whether the student has formed his opinion on such subjects like "Patriotism", "Habits", "Essentials of character" etc. He is set topics on abstracts as well as on social, political and domestic affairs. Current and problematic issues such as "Food Froblem", "Rising Prices" are set to test information.

(4) **Expository Essays.** In an expository essay, we have to explain a thing or to establish the truth of a statement to make others believe. The proverbial statements like "The child is the father of man", "Sweets are the uses of adversity", or subjects like "Co-education", "Fashions", "Pleasures of Reading", "Nationalism" and "Internationalism" are set from this category. It is essential the views both for and against the proposition should be advanced and concluded.

(5) **Imaginary Essays.** In an imaginative essay the writer has to imagine himself in a certain situation at a certain point of time. Such topics as "What will they say", "The shape of things to come", "India of my dreams" are from this category. Extreme care must be exercised in planning such essays. Imitation of any short must be avoided.

THE PRE-REQUISITES OF ESSAY WRITING

Mathew Arnold spoke the truth about essay writing, "Have something to say and say it as clearly as you can. Nothing high or too low for an essay. No statement is special to the essay, nor alien to it except judicious handling and arrangements of thoughts. A student must know about all what is exactly wanted to him and how he can go.

An essay is a string of thoughts artistically arranged. It is a pity that modern student just starts off the essay after writing the title on the page of the answer book. As the sentences appear in his mind, he puts them one after the other. It is fruitful to devote some time thinking over pros and cons of the matter and write down the points as they appear. In first place principal ideas must be taken down. Pruning of the material is essential; for it grants exactness and accuracy to writing.

It is not a mark of intelligence to go against the topic. However, any contradiction if at all indulged in must be supported by convincing arguments. Worn-out and hacknayed statements must be avoided.

The introduction and conclusion must be attractive and convincing. It is with the very first sentence that the student invites and attracts the attention of the examiner. Again carefully worded conclusion is bound to secure more marks. However, the body of essay is not to be filled in with superfluous padding material.

Moreover, it is also essential that the writing is neatly divided into paragraphs. Straight forwardness pleasant-tone, clarity of thought and lucidity of expression constitute the qualities of good essay writing.

The length of an essay should not exceed the limit prescribed in the question paper. In case of the Secondary School Examination generally, the limit does not exceed 250 words. A good essay is brief, to the point lucid, direct and clear.

GENERAL HINTS ON ESSAY WRITING

While writing an essay we should keep the following points in view :

(1) Try to understand the topic. It is absolutely necessary, otherwise, you may waste much time and paper.

(2) Think over the topic sometime and make and outline of the ideas you wish to express is your essay.

(3) Bearing the subject in mind arrange all the ideas in their proper order from the brief introduction to conclusion.

(4) Keep strictly to your points and write a separate paragraph on each point. Take care that next paragraph appears to be well connected with the previous one.

(5) The beginning and the ending must be striking.

(6) Write from your own knowledge and observations.

(7) Be brief and to the point. Do not use big words and lengthy sentences.

(8) Revise your essay and correct all grammatical and spelling mistakes.

MY FAVOURITE LEADERS

MAHATMA GANDHI

Mahatma Gandhi's name is on the lips of everybody. He was the greatest man only of India but of the world also. He was the father of the nation. We generally call him Bapu.

Mahatma Gandhi was born at Porbandar in Kathiawar in the year of 1869 on 2nd October. His father, Kaba Gandhi was the Diwan of Rajkot State. His mother was a noble and pious lady.

At the age of seven he was sent to school. At school he proved himself to be only an average boy. He was always regular and punctual in his class. After passing his Matriculation Examination he studied at college. Then he went to England to study law.

He started his practice at Bombay. But he did not do well. Then he went to Rajkot. He was not a successful lawyer.

He went to Africa to conduct a big law suit in a court. There he saw the bad condition of Indians. He put up a brave fight for their rights. He founded Natal Indian Congress. He was jailed with his friends. In 1914 the Indian Relief Act was passed. This bettered the lot of Indians.

Gandhi returned to India. He joined the Congress. He became its leader. Under his leadership the Congress started non-violence and non-cooperation movements to oppose the unjust acts of the British Government. Side by side he did constructive work-the removal of untouchability and the Hindu-Muslim Unity. At last India became free on the 15th of August 1947.

Gandhiji's end came all a sudden. He was shot dead by a thoughtless youngman. He died on 30th January, 1948.

Gandhiji was deeply religious man. He taught and practised truth. He lived a very simple life. He had great love for the poor. He followed the path of truth and Ahinsa. He was a great saint.

Gandhiji was a great teacher, preacher, thinker and a soldier. He will be remembered and respected by the world of ever. The finest tribute paid to him was from General Smute who called him "a prince among men."

May his soul rest in piece! May his teachings show the right path to humanity of the day!

PANDIT JAWAHAR LAL NEHRU

All of us have heard his name. He was our first Prime Minister. He was known all over the world.

Shri Nehru was born at Allahabad in 1889 on 14th November. His father Motilal Nehru was a great lawyer. He brought up his son as a prince. Very efficient teachers taught him.

At the age of 15, he was sent to England for higher studies. There he joined the Public School at Harrow. Then he went to the Cambridge University where he took his degree in 1910. Then he joined law. He was called to Bar in

1912. He came to India. He started his practice at Allahabad High Court. He was married at the age of 27.

In the young age of Nehruji the British ruled over India. The English treated Indians badly. This pained the heart of Jawahar Lal Nehru. He gave up practice. He joined the Non-co-operation Movement started by Gandhiji. He went to jail several times. He bore punishments happily. But jail life could not crush his spirit. He struggled bravely. He acted as Congress President in four different years before India became free. When India became free, he was elected the first Prime Minister of India.

Pt. Nehru was a successful Prime Minister. India made great progress under his guidance. Dr. Rajinder Prasad, our late President, once said, "the country is marching forward on the road of progress in the leadership of Panditji." He did a lot for the world. Had he lived some years more, the country would have become very strong. He solved some difficult problems of the country as well as the world.

China attacked India in 1962. This attack told upon his health. He never expected that China would prove tracherous. He had heart attack on 27th May, 1964 and he passed away from this world.

Nehruji was a great statesman. He was good writer and speaker. He wrote many famous books. He was great friend of the poor. He was the servant of the people. He lived for the good of this country. He loved justice and truth. He could not bear opposition.

Nehru was a truc lover of peace. He laid down five principles called 'Punch Shila'. May his soul find place in Paradise!

SUBHASH CHANDRA BOSE

Subhash Chandra Bose was one of the greatest leaders of India. He is famous by the name of Netaji. He gave up his life for his motherland. His death is a great loss to the country.

Subhash Chandra Bose was born on 23rd January, 1897 in Cuttack. His father was famous lawyer. He came of a very well-to-do family.

Even as a child he showed signs of future greatness. He was a very brilliant boy at school. He beat a European professor of his school. He was turned out from the school.

He passed the Matriculation Examination from Cuttack. Then he joined the Presidency College, Calcutta. He passed his B.A. from another college in the first division. Then he went to England and took the Tripose degree from Cambridge University. He also passed the I.C.S. Examination. But he was not interested in becoming a high official. He wished to serve his country. So he resigned from I.C.S.

He joined the Congress movement to serve the cause of the freedom of his country. He belonged to the Forward Block of the Congress. In 1939 he was elected President of the Congress. As he had differences with Gandhiji. He resigned the Presidentship.

He escaped from India during the Second World War. He went to Germany to seek help. Hitler received him warmly and promised all possible help. He gave Netaji military training for two years. Now he became a good General.

While in Germany, he raised the Indian National Army from amongst the Indian prisoners of war. He came to Japan to be nearer India. Here he also raised the army. Other Indians of Far East joined his army. The morale and discipline of the army were excellent.

With his army he started towards India. He attacked India from the side of Assam. He got a little success in the beginning. But Germany and Japan fell soon after. He flew in Japan. But his plane crashed on the way and he died.

Though Netaji is no more in this world, yet his name will ever shine. He will always be counted the greatest martry of the country. He used to say, "Give me your blood, I promise you freedom".

SARDAR VALLABH BHAI PATEL : THE IRON MAN OF INDIA

Our Motherland is always fulfill with her brave and great sons and daughters. These great persons give the pride to our country and also make ourself famous in such way of the people of the next generation learn them with honour. Sardar Vallabh Bhai Patel was a great son of our Motherland. He was born on 31st October 1875 in Karamsad village of the Khera district in Gujrat. His father was an ordinary farmer. He had to face a lot of difficulties but he overcomed them all and made a great lawyer. But he first came to light in the Bardoli Farmer Satyagraha in 1928. He was first meet

Mahatma Gandhi in this movement and Mahatma Gandhi was very much impressed with his talent of leadership and his courage. In this movement Mahatma Gandhi gave him the title Sardar. In 1930 he was elected the President of Congress.

In all the movements of Indian freedom Sardar Patel played an active role and after the Independent he became the Deputy Prime Minister and the Home Minister of India, there one important point is that twelve out of fifteen provincial committees of Congress party support in favour of the Prime Ministership of Sardar Patel. But Mahatma Gandhi wanted to Pt. Nehru because the Prime Minister so Sardar Patel honously accepted Gandhiji's proposal.

After Independent and soverign states into one flag. Now, this was the challange before win and he accepted and do their duty well and delete the Independence of all sovereign states without any fighting or war. The power used by him only over the Nizam of Hyderabad. He also wanted to preserve our national heritedge and pride he reconstructed the world famous temple of Somnath in Nov. 1947 after 923 years when Mehmood Gaznabi demolished it. Above all we can say that what he did for our country which is extremely great and no other people can do so. He is called the Iron Man of India and this title classified him alongwith the great personality of Germany Bismark, because Bismark did the same job for Germany which Mr. Patel did for India. He leave this world on 15th December 1950. At last we can say that he was the great son of our Motherland.

MOTHER TERESA

Mother Teresa is considered to be a moving angel on the earth. A simple old missionary lady is known today throughout the world. She is the saviour of thousands of orphans and deserted children. At the time of her birth she was called Agnes. Her father was a farmer at Spoji in Yogoslavia on August 27, 1910. A brother and a sister younger to her were also in that family. She was the eldest. Instead of marriage she preferred to join as a nun in the Roman Catholic Church. With the consent of her parents she was admitted as a sister of the Roman Catholic Church. She joined service of the Church and came to India when she was just 19 years, on 6 January, 1929.

Miss Agnes was named as Sister Teresa and assigned to work as a teacher at Calcutta. She was not happy to continue as a teacher. She saw in the streets of Calcutta poverty, sickness and misery. Number of children were seen deserted and there were many orphans. They had none to care for. There were many sick and miserable persons. She wanted to serve them.

Having only Rs. 5/- with her, she took a small room and started serving them. She took care of the deserted children. She also nursed the sick. She started a small school. Seeing the selfless service undertaking by a foreign lady, many ladies in Calcutta joined her. Thus came into being the institution called Missionaries of Charity. Sister Teresa never went back to her motherland. With many sisters joining her organisation Sister Teresa became Mother Teresa.

As years passed by, Mother Teresa expanded her missionary activities to other cities and to other countries too. Missionaries of charity, today, are seen in almost all big cities of India. Her institutions are now doing service in Srilanka, Australia and even in far away countries like Venizula.

Love and compassion are the cordinal principles of her mission. Serving the needy and the poor is serving God, she says. Her will power and dedication to the cause of poor and to the cause of destitute children has earned her national recognition. Mother Teresa has been honoured by many awards, Raman Magsay Award (1962), Jawahar Lal Nehru (1972), International Award of Peace (1973), Templeton Foundation Award (1979), Bharat Ratna (1980), for noble work.

Today Mother Teresa is a moving symbol of Love and Compassion. She is spreading the message of Love of Lord Jesus in all corners of the Globe. She has chosen India as her country. She is now Mother General in her mission. Subhashini Das who was the first disciple of Mother Teresa, is now Sister Agnes.

MRS. INDIRA GANDHI

Mrs. Indira Gandhi was the beloved leader of the people of India. To see her was to love her. After her downfall 1977, the people had again placed the country in her hands in 1980.

She was born on November 19, 1917. She was brought up in a family full of political activities and love of country.

So the family atmosphere had a great influence on her mind. She got her education at Allahabad, Oxford and Shanti Niketan. In 1942, she was married to Mr. Feroz Gandhi, a Parsi Youth. He died in 1960, she had two sons—Rajiv and Sanjay.

Indira Gandhi was the worthy daughter of a worthy father. She was a born politician. After the death of her mother she had a very difficult time. In her early life she jumped into politics. She had been the member of Indian National Congress. In 1959 she was elected President of N. Congress. It was only after the death of her father that she became the Minister of Information and Broadcasting. After the untimely death of Sh. Lal Bahadur Shastri in 1966 she was elected Prime Minister of India.

She held the great office for about 17 years. During her period of reign she led the country to a place of honour. It was under her leadership in 1971, that India defeated Pakistan and broke its back for ever. She nationalised all the major banks and abolished privy purses. These were two bold steps. In 1975 the opposition parties revolted after the historical judgment of Justice Sinha. To put all opposition down she declared a state of Internal Emergency. This brought her defeat in the general election of 1977. She was in hot water for a period of two and a half years. In the mid-term poll, held in January 1980 she won back her lost position.

On the black Wednesday morning of 31st October, 1984, at 9-18 A.M. she was shot dead at her residence by two of her own security guards named Beant Singh and Satwant Singh. She died after few hours.

The nation mourned her death. In her death the nation lost a worthy maker of India.

Dr. A. P. J. ABDUL KALAM

Abul Paker Janual Abeden Abdul Kalam became the 12th Presedent of the republic of India. He was elected with more then 90% votes more then the other candidate who was captain Laxmi Sehgal supported by Left Parties, Dr. Kalam gets the support from the NDA and Congress.

Dr. Kalam was borned on 15th October 1931 in Rameshwaram of Tamil Nadu. His father was an ordinery man who gave the boats on rent to fishermen. He was the big favoures of self independence and self respect. He helped his family economically with selling newspapers. Kalam completed B.Sc. from Sent Josephs College of Trichanapalli. After that he taking engineering degree in Aronotical Engineering from IIT Chennai. He joined DRDO (Defence Ressaren and Development Organisation) in 1958. After that he worked on the missile programmes run by ISRO (Indian Space Research Organisation) from 1962 to 1982. He became the director of DRDO in 1982 and worked on Integrated Directed Missile Programme. He also worked over the project on Agni Missile and Arjun Tank and also on high compact Aircraft. After that he received "Bharat Ratna" award in 1997 and before this he got Padam Vibhushan in 1990 and Padam Bhushan in 1981.

After all this achievements he was elected the President of India on 25th July 2002.

He was called the title of "Missile Man" because he was the most responsible man for the missile and weapons programmes. He also contribute a lot in the atomic programme of India. He was first came into light when India done their first atomic blast on 24th June 1974 and after this he was the main person behind the Atomic blasts on 11th and 13th April 1999 which is called "Operation Vijay" by Prime Minister Atal Bihari Vajpayee.

Dr. Kalam is example of self confidence labour, ambition and patriotism. Dr. Kalam loves to play veena, he is an unmarried man and he also vegiterion completely. He was a President who has a lot of qualitics such as :

(1) He was never be the member of any political party.

(2) He was the first scientist who reach on this post.

(3) He never participate in any type of assembly or parliament election before he elected the President.

(4) He was not selected the Dr. President, he was the fourth person who elected President without electing Dr. President.

ATAL BIHARI VAJPAYEE : A SUCCESSFUL PRIME MINISTER

In Indian Democratic setup Govt. the post of Prime Minister is the most important post. We have a lot of good Prime Ministers like Pandit Nehru, Indira Gandhi, Rajeev Gandhi. Now the Prime Minister of India Mr. Atal Bihari Vajpayee is a very experienced and tallented man. He was born in Gwalior (M.P.) on 25th December 1925. He first time elected the member of Parliament in 1957 after that he regularly touched with politics, the elected member of Parliament ten times. Now in 1996 he got the first chance to because a Prime Minister on 15th May because BJP was the biggest party but he can't proved his majority in Lok Sabha so he resigned on 28th May 1996.

After this he got chance in 1998 and he ruled over country about 12 months after that a non-confidence proposal put into Lok Sabha and his Govt. failed from one vote and another mid-term election we had to face. In 1999 BJP before elections made group of parties and named this group NDA (National Democratic Alliance) and this group elected Vajpayee their leader so in 1999 NDA gets absolute majority and Vajpayee became the Prime Minister of India third time. Now Vajpayee very carefully and strongly regulate the Govt. At this time NDA has 24 Political Parties and Vajpayee is able to get them together and works it shows the talent and political experience of our Prime Minister. Vajpayee visits to many countries make our relations better with them and the successful foreign policy of him improve the image of our country infront of the world. Vajpayee always ready to solve any matter or problem with peace and his this policy is now fulfilling today when the Air, Rail and Bus links with Pakistan is again regular and also the cricket relations maintain again Vajpayee always ready to do better for the farmers, labours and poor people of India. He starts the Crop Insurance and poor people of India. He starts the Crop Insurance Scheme for the farmers and the Insurance Scheme for the labourers of unorganised sector. In these scheme Govt. of India pay half amount of the premium and half pay by the farmer and labourer think very carefully that our country must reach the mark of a develop nation as soon as possible. He is an unmarried man he is also a good poet. He is a popular leader in India as well as in World. The public of Pakistan loves the poems of Vajpayee and honour him as a great leader. At least we can say that he is a good leader and good Prime Minister and we can make our country develop very soon under his leadership.

OUR FESTIVALS

THE DUSSEHRA FESTIVAL

Dussehra is the most important Hindu festival. It is performed for ten days throughout the country. The festival is celebrated for the victory good over evil. It comes in the second fortnight of the month of "Asauj" according to lunar calender and in the month of October of English calender every year.

Dussehra is so called because it is celebrated for ten days. It is also said Dussehra represents ten days of penance for removing ten different sins. In the Northern parts of the country, it is performed as "Nav Ratri" or Durga Pooja festivals. For nine days and nights goddess Durga fought with several Demons and came out victoriously on the ninth day, the tenth day is called Vijayadasami or victorious tenth day. On this day jubiliation, joy and happiness is shared amongest all the Hindus. Thus this festival is performed mainly on three days. The eighth day as "Durga Asthami" and the ninth day as "Mahanavami" and the tenth victorious day as "Vijayadasami". Yet another reason for celebrating this festival is Pandavas exile of living incognito was over on this day.

During these festive days, the epic story of Ramayana is depicted throughout North in the form of ballets, stage shows, dramas popularly known as "Rama Lilas". The children are always eager to go in the night to see such dramas and they enjoy and learn a great deal of life of Rama, his mission, his truthful nature, his duty and noble character. Thus on the final day, that is the day of victory—effigies of Ravana, Khumbh Karan and Meghnath are burnt with a fine display of fire works. The whole Ramalila ground of every city, Town and Public place is filled with men, women and children. A big fair is arranged, fine lighting and gay festive show brings lots of pleasure hustle bustle, fun and frolic, mirth and gaiety in the environs.

In Bengal idols of goddess Durga are made. These beautiful idols are worshipped for nine days. The rituals of the last three days Durga Ashtami, Mahanavmi and Vijayadasami are most important days of the function. On the last day, these idols are taken out in the form of procession with Prayers, Bhajans and Kirtans to be immersed in rivers or lakes. In South India performance of "Devi Nav Ratans" or worship of goddess Durga for nine days is done at several temples, public places and houses. In each of the South Indian homes assortation of dolls and images into lively and imaginative way to please the eyes; and people take pride in exhibiting rich and great artistic taste in arranging "Courts of Dolls".

On the main festival day people take bath and perform religious worship of goddess Durga in the houses and temples. Vehicles and arms are also worshipped in certain parts of the country. They take festive food prepared deliciously in the houses, wear new clothes, and visit temples. They move out joyfully meeting friends and relatives and exchange greeting with all in a pleasureful way.

It is a festival of triumph of good over evil. Probably it is one of the most important festival where religious, social and cultural sentiments are exhibited trying the whole country into a single unit.

DEEPAWALI

Deepawali or Dewali is one of the most important festival of Hindus. It is the most rejoining festival of India. Deepawali literally means rows of lighted lamps. **On the day** of festival every house of a Hindu is illuminated with lights. Thus Diwali is a festival of lighted lamps enjoyed by all.

It is performed on new moon day in the month of Kartik every year by Hindu calander. Generally the festival falls in between middle of October to middle of November according to English calender.

There are several views behind the celebration of this festival. In certain parts of India Deepawali is associated with goddess Lakshmi. It is believed on this day Lord Vishnu freed Lakshmi (goddess of wealth) from king Bali. Yet another popular version is that on this day King Rama returned to Ayodya after victoriously killing Ravana, after fourteen years of exile. Another view prevalent in many parts of South India is that Lord Krishna with the help of his spouse Satya Bhama slew the demon king Naraka on 'Chathurdasi' a day prior to new moon day. That is why this day is celebrated as victory day of Lord Krishna. Allmost all the Hindus believe on this day goddess Lakshmi, the diety of wealth and prosperity visits every house. So to welcome her the houses are illuminated throughout the night.

The reason behind the festival perhaps is the social good. The months of October, November have the darkest nights. In the days gone be to show the way for those on high seas and for general lighting of villages, towns and cities. This festival might have come into existance. Whatever the reason is, it is a festival of joy and pleasure.

Preparation are made several weeks ahead of the festive day. White-washing and painting the shops and houses are made much earlier to the festival. All the waste, jenk and debris are thrown away. The house are washed and cleaned thoroughly. Rooms are decorated with new pictures of dieties and beautiful sceneries. Furniture and other articles are also well polished. Special sweets saltish savouries are prepared for the festival. Delicious food is prepared for the ceremonial occasion.

On *"Dhan Theras"* the thirteenth day of waning moon new utensils are purchased. It is considered auspicious of buy new utensils on this day. So hundreds of shops of utensils brilliantly lighted and decorated for this occasion are opened.

Crowds of people gather round these shops to purchase utensils.

Also several shops of selling fire crackes and other fire works are also opened. The pyrotechnics of these shops is worth seeing. They attract and lure young and youth. Several lakhs worth of fire works are purchased in the cities of India.

Shops and roadside hawkers selling candles, earthen-lamp, cotton for wicks, oil and many other decorating items can be seen on the streets of any city and town throughout India on the day.

In North India the emphasis is more on illumination where as in South India it is on both pyrotechnics and lighting.

The next day is called as *"Choti Diwali"* in the Northern parts of India where as in south it is called *"Nanak Chathurdasi"*. Earthenlamps with wick and oil are lit and worshipped and display of fire works in a very small scale is done at the night of this day. Young children feel happy throughout the months of October, November because of Durga Pooja, Rama Lila, Celebrations and finally the festival of Diwali with sweets and fire works. Cracking sounds of a toy pistol or some other sounds and shoots can be heard during these festival days.

Traders and Merchants start their new account books closing the old on this day. Most of the Jewellary shops, business houses are opened on this day and several sweet-shops do roaring business.

On the day of Amavasya, Diwali main festival is performed with pomp and show. Every person rich and poor purchases sweets according to their status, lit the earthenlamps with oil and wick, candles or electric bulbs small and big, coloured and decoration lamps. Elders and youngsters, women and men wear new clothes, young boys and youth display their fire work in sportive competition. Sounds of pyrotechnics can be heard all most upto midnight on that day. The lady of the house performs Lakshmi Pooja or worship of goddess Lakshmi. The men folk in some houses gamble the whole night. Perhaps with the belief that if they win on that night they will be successful throughout that year. In this way the festival of lamps, joy and jubiliation comes to a close with exchange of sweets and greetings.

The festival has many advantages. The first being the cleaning and white-washing of houses. The festival encourages potters who make earthenware lamps and manufacturers of fire works and utensils. The Sulphur fumes kill the microbes and virus. The decoration of shops and houses provides relief to the eyes and gladen the hearts.

The festival has some disadvantages, the first one being gambling and the second the injuries sustained by those who explode fire crackers etc.

THE HOLI

Holi is the festival of colours. It is a festival of gaiety and glamour. It brings joy and relaxation to young and old, rich and poor equally.

It falls on the full moon day of the month of Phalgun every year by Hindu calendar and in the month of March according to the English calender.

There are several reasons behind its celebration. The popular one is that Prahlad, son of Hiranya Kashyap—a demon king was a very good devotee of God. Where as the father was an enemy of God and believed in his own power. The demon king tried his best to teach Prahlad hatred towards God. Prahlad never deviated from his path of devotion of God. The king tried in vain to kill his own son by biting him with serpents, by crushing him (trampling) under the feet of elephants, by throwing him from high hills and by roasting him in boiling oil. Every time he was saved by grace of Lord Vishnu whom Prahlad believed with mind, soul and body.

The king being vexed in his attempts to kill his enemy's devotee consulted his sister Holika. She was gifted with the boon that fire can not burn her. On the order of king that she sat in fire with Prahalad on her lap. By the grace of God once more Prahlad survived and Holika burnt to ashes. This happened on the full moon day of Phalgun. To commemorate the occasion of the burning of evil forces this festival is celebrated the next day with jubiliation and joy.

According to another epic tale that Lord Shiva was involved in severe penance on the top of Himalayan mountains. Kamdeo (Love-god or Man math) along with Rathi—the god couple of sex and love tried to induce passion and desire in the heart of Lord Shiva. But Lord Shiva who was disturbed in penance opened his third eye and burnt the Kamdeo into ashes on the full moon day of Phalgun month. But Lord Shiva was merciful enough to once more revive him to life because of the prayers of Rathi. To celebrate this pleasureful occasion Holi is performed as Kamdeo festival in some parts of South.

Prior to celebration of the festival, people collect in different mohallahs heaps wood, logs, Dung cakes etc. On the day of festival women perform worship in the houses and Holi is burnt in the night according to ritualistic procedure. People worship the fire and parch green cars of barley and gram in it. Latter the parched material is distributed among friends and relatives.

The jubiliation and joyful part of the festival is celebrated on the next day morning on wards. People throw coloured waters made out of flower and roots in earlier times. This now changed to waters of chemical colours. Young children and youth join in this playful colour water sprinking. The elderly people apply gulal (red vermilon powder) to each others forehead and embrace each other. After that they enjoy the play of youth of young.

Dances, songs throwing coloured water on each other in a gay mood is one of the most main attraction of this festival.

In this festival, old enemities are burried and people start fresh and friendly relations. People of all the classes and castes and creeds join this festival with a open heart of love and affection. The Holi play continues till mid noon. They take bath eat festive food in the houses and come in the evening for Holi milan—then they sprink dry colours only on each other. Holi milan—friends and relatives embrace each other with exchange of Holi greetings. Exchange of sweets, fruits and good wishes is usually done on this festival.

It is one of the finest festivals where gaiety, colours, love and joy pours forth from the bottom of human heart without grudge or grumbling from rich and poor, old and young and men and women alike.

RAKSHA BANDHAN

This is a festival of importance for Hindus. A vow to protect the right and justice in the society is taken on this festival day.

The festival falls on the full-moon day in the month of Shrawan by Hindu calender and in the month of August according to English calender. Rains cool the atmosphere. Moon light provides a pleasant and peaceful environment.

In the times gone by brahmins, sages and seers who were meek physically but mentally strong, were always in need of protection from the physical danger. Kshatriyas were the protectors of the whole society. They were always ready to use their sword in protection of the weak and wise. Gurus, well red Brahmins and men of hermitages used to tie a holy thread on the wrists of kings, brave and strong men. This thread, tied by the learned people, is a symbol of blessing and vow to their life and safety. This thread always reminded the kings and the brave to protect those who tied it one their wrists. It functioned as a safety shield, gave them strength and inspired to protect weak and uphold right and justice in the society.

At present the pundits and purohits tie on the wrists of nobles rich and strong. In return they get some money, clothes or some other gratification.

This custom of asking protection, during Muslim invasion shifted to woman folk. The household woman tied the holy thread called Rakhi—the one who protects, on the wrists of their brothers. Now, this thread is mainly as symbol of brother-sister relationship. It is tied to the wrist of brother by sister. The brother takes the vow to protect her modesty, chastity and life. History tells that Humayun protected Rani Karnavati of Mewar from the invasion of Shersha Suri when he received Rakhi thread from Karnavati. Every year this festival reminds us of pure and pious relation between brother and sister. Blessings from the heart of sister to the safety and well being of her brother are put in this thread. That is why this "Raksha Bandhan" possess importance and purity.

One day prior to festival, something in yellow or red is drawn in the house which is called 'sona'. For this occasion Milk pudding with rice (Khir) and vermicelli (Semai) are cooked. These items are offered to sona and Rakhi. After the worship, the sisters in the house tie Rakhi thread to wrists of brothers and apply tilak to their forehead. Brothers provided to the sisters money or clothes or both according to the capacity and desire. Then all the family members sit together to eat pucca food cooked by the lady of the house alongwith semai and khir. Barley ears grown for this occasion in an earthen pot are also given by sister to the brothers and rest they immerse in the rivers or lakes.

Raksha Bandhan is a festival of strong protecting the weak. It is the most important festival to remind the brother-sister relationship to the whole world. Every brother should feel proud and take vow to protect his sisters.

INDEPENDENCE DAY

The 15th August is the most important day in the history of India. On this day our country became free after many centuries.

We celebrate this day with great zeal every year. This year we made great preparations in our school. Everyone of us eager to take part in the Independence Day Celebrations. The Vice Principal drew up a programme. It was announced by the Principai on the 12th of August.

Early in the morning of the 15th of August we gathered in the Ramleela ground behind the bus stand near the water tank. Our teachers also joined us in a few minutes. We were divided into four parties. Each party singing national songs and shouting *'Bapu Gandhi ki Jai'*, *'Bharat Mata ki Jai'*. Our younger companions were full of more enthusiasm. They were shouting the slogans at top of their voice. Thus, singing and shouting national slogans we reached school at 8.00 a.m.

In the school we stood round the flag pole. The teachers asked us to stand classwise. In our *Khaki* uniform we looked like soldiers ready to give our lives for the sake Mother India. The teachers stood behind us. On our Principal's request the founder of the school, who is a scared saint, came forward. He performed the flag hosting ceremony. He was in his happy mood. Exactly at 8.30 o'clock the flag was hoisted. We stood in attention to give salute to the flag.

After the flag ceremony *'Jan Gan Man'* was sung. The scout band played the tune. The flag ceremony came to a close with a few speeches. The teachers and the founder delivered these speeches. All the speakers threw light on the importance of the day. Two teachers told us our duties towards the country.

The Principal asked us to assemble round the field to take part in the sports. The sports were held with great zeal. Those who stood first and second in the sports got prizes by the holy hands of the founder.

TEACHER'S DAY

Teacher's Day is a national function, celebrated only in India. It is held on September 5th of every year which is also the birthday of Dr. Sarvepalli Radhakrishnan, one of our former President Dr. Radhakrishnan was an ideal teacher. So it was decided to celebrate his birthday as Teacher's Day to honour that noble profession.

The main idea is to draw the attention of the society towards this profession. No other profession, either medical or legal, have a day meant to celebrate and honour the best among them. It is a unique honour awarded to the teaching profession in our country.

On that day nearly a hundred teachers selected from primary, upper primary and secondary schools, oriental schools and colleges are invited by the President of India and honoured by giving a certificate of recognition along with some cash prize. The award given by the President is called the National Award for Teachers, which is a great honour to the humble teachers. Selection for these awards are made on the basis of many considerations. Teacher's personal character and conduct, his professional competence, his sociability, the results he produced, the contribution he made to the profession as a writer, and as a researcher in Education, the popularity he enjoys in public, his efforts to eradicate illiteracy, public support he got for building infrastructure to his institution etc. The part he plays in extracurricular activities is also taken into account. So it not easy to get a national award. Only ideal and worthy teachers can get it.

Besides National awards, State awards and awards by National Foundation for teachers are also given. In some districts, district level awards are also given to encourage ideal teachers. Giving an award is a good incentive.

Of late the awards given by government have become mechanical. The original idea of involving the society at large, to recognise this noble profession is missing. Many functions are being arranged by teachers to honour their fellow teachers. The parents are not showing the expected interest.

It was true, that a teacher enjoyed a place of honour after the mother and father and was only next to them, in our ancient society. Many changes have taken place. A teacher is no longer a selfless Guru. He is a paid employee, just like any other worker in an office or factory. With this social concept, it is difficult to expect the society to honour the teachers. But even now there are teachers who are respected and loved for their selfless service, spotless character and unbiased love and affection they show to their students. All such teachers may not get awards. The social respect they command is itself an award. As Dr. S. Radhakrishnan had himself said, teaching is its own reward. The satisfaction it gives the teacher is not comparable. A good teacher is always remembered by the student wherever he is.

THE CHILDREN'S DAY

The 14th November is called the Children's Day. On this day Pt. Jawahar Lal Nehru was born. He was the first Prime Minister of free India. He had a great love for children. They too loved him greatly and called him 'Chacha Nehru'. The Children' Day is celebrated on 14th November as a mark of his love for children. It is celebrated all over India.

In our school, it was celebrated with great enthusiasm. On 12th November the student's representatives had a meeting with the Principal. It was decided that the children will run the school from Top to Bottom on 14th November. Only the clerk office will be maintained by the original persons. The school representatives invited the names from the students to work in different capacities. All was decided a day earlier. The posts of the Principal and Vice Principal were handled by senior class students. The Principal held the meeting of his staff a day earlier and instructed to keep watch on the students so that the discipline of the school might not be disturbed.

Next morning, a student who was acting as a peon rang the bell. All the students went to their classes. The acting staff and acting Principal were in different dress. The acting class teachers went to their respective classes and took the roll call. At the second bell, the students came out of their classes and began to move to the morning assembly. Another student acting as physical education teacher successfully conducted the assembly. As usual morning prayer was recited and a student read out the news. Then the acting Principal gave some important instructions to the students. The physical education teacher, then, asked the students to do some exercises. The students, then, moved to their classes in a line.

All the acting subjects teachers took their classes. It was amazing to see that the students were co-operating them fully. The subject teachers were taking the classes confidently. Some of them were imitating their old subject teachers. This imitation made their lesson more interesting. Occasionally, the acting Principal used to take rounds to check any mischief committed by students. The original staff was free for the whole day.

The school closed as usual at 3.30 p.m. It was very remarkable to see that the students were moving towards the gate in a disciplined manner. The Principal and other teachers congratulated the acting staff for their good show. It became the talk of the town. No untoward happening took place.

SCIENCE AND TECHNOLOGY
SCIENCE IN EVERYDAY LIFE

The age in which we are living is the age of science. It has added to out power to such an extent that it has become possible for us to triumph over and shape our physical environments. The inexhaustible material gifts of science have alreay added much to our health, resources and power.

Science has made fairy-tales sounds real. Today, we can speak to a friend in London. Medical science has added much to our relief. Surgery has helped in saving millions of human lives. Electricity is the maid of all work. It lights our houses, cooks our food, and does all our washing.

Science has introduced new means of entertainment. We can listen to sweet music and hear the talks of distinguished men from all over the world. Cinema is not only the source of recreation but also of much educational value.

The invention of printing press has enabled us to have an easy access to the books which help us in broadening our outlook and sharpening our intellect. The newspapers bring us the news from all over the world.

Now, we have grown logical and methodical. Science, no doubt, has brought about miraculous changes in our life, and has provided us with all sorts of amenities. It has enriched us materially but has improverished us in spirit. Human affection, love and sentiments have been completely crushed. Selfishness and greed have taken a high hold upon us.

SCIENCE AS A CURSE

Modern age is an age of science. Science has brought about a revolution in the life of man. It has made life easier and comfortable. It has conquered time and distance. It has played a great role incuring deadly diseases. It has revolutionised industry and agriculture. It has landed man on the moon. Artificial satellites provide information in advance. Science is thus the best friend of man.

At the same time, science has proved to be the worst enemy of man. It has become a threat to human existence. It has done the greatest dis-service to man in the field of armaments. It has given deadly and destructive weapons of war. Science has become a terrible menace or danger.

It was in the fifteenth century that gun-powder was invented. Since then, it has been adding to the store of deadly weapons and explosions. Not only dictators but even democratic rulers look upon science as their most reliably in war. It has become the handmaid of modern state. Scientists are working for monetary gains to discover new formula for killing the largest number of human beings in the shortest possible time. Science can rightly be called the murderer of humanity.

Science has produced very effective pistols, automatic assault rifles, recoilless guns. Then there are armoured cars, tanks and cannons. Tanks are just like moving fortresses. They are being modernised everyday. They let lose a rain of fire within miles.

Then there are bombs of various types. Hand grenades are the most elementary things. There are napalm bombs that cause burns. Second world war witnessed atom-bombs. One bomb each was dropped on Hiroshima and Nagasaki by America. It killed thousands and thousands of people with a radius of ten miles. The present atom-bombs are more deadly and destructive. Hydrogen bomb is even more destructive than an atom bomb. America has invented even neutron bomb.

These bomb rain hell over earth. They are carried by bombers. There are various types of bombers with the latest equipment. America has F-16's while Soviet Russia has MIG-29. Even during Second World War, Hitler would send hundreds of planes that would cast their shade on London.

Then there are rockets and missiles. They may be described as flying bombs. They fly themselves. No aeroplanes are required to drop them. There are inter-continental Ballistic Missiles and medium range Ballistic Missiles. The inter-continanatal missiles fly thousands of miles to hit a fixed target. Washington can hit Mascow and vice versa. No place is secure these days. There are anti-Ballistic Missiles also. Nuclear powered sub-marines given a new dimension to war tone.

It is, however, no fault of science. It is the fault of man. It depends upon him as to what purpose he wants science to serve. Man should mend himself. Science will be at the service of mankind.

IS SCIENCE A FRIEND OR AN ENEMY?

Modern age is an age of science. Science has brought about a revolution in the life of man. It has made life easier and comfortable. On the other hand, science has proved to be the worst enemy of man. It has given deadly and destructive weapons of war. It has become a terrible danger.

The question now being asked is whether science is a blessing or a curse.

Those who regard science as a curse, think only of bombers, missiles, atomic and hydrogen bombes, tanks and submarines. They do not think of a thousand other things created by science for the benefit of man. They give comfort and delight to mankind. We have only to think of electricity, telephone, telegraph, wireless, steam engine, aeroplane, X-rays etc. They have all contributed to the making of present day civilisation.

Science has given us electricity. We use it in our homes, factories, workshops, cinema halls and everywhere. It is with the help of electricity that all other appliances and machines work. It runs even the tubewells of farmers.

Science has placed at our disposal cinema, radio and television. All of them provide pleasure to the weary mind. The television brings into our homes the joyful and interesting sciences and activities of the outside world.

Science is the greatest saviour of man. Everyday, it pulls out of the jaws of death thousands of persons. The science of medicine and the science of surgery perform miracles. Surgery not only cures heart disease but gives eyesight to the blind and limbs to the limbless.

There is no denying the fact that science is also working for the destruction of our civilisation. Atom bomb and hydrogen bomb are the greatest danger. They can destroy mankind within minutes. Everything will be reduced to ashes.

But we should remember that it is the use to which science is put, makes it as our friend or enemy. Atomic energy, of which we are so afraid, is a great blessing. It can increase the produce of the soil. It can cure cancer. Atomic energy can take the place of coal and petrol. They are on the verge of extinction. Atomic energy is the greatest friend of man if used for peaceful purposes.

So, science is not a curse. It is a friend of man. It is a blessing. This is the duty of man to put it to proper use. Science should not be blamed for the insanity of man.

SCIENCE AND CIVILIZATION

Science has altered the world by list of wonderful discoveries and inventions. There have been brought about in the world many revolutionary changes which would have been impossible but for science. It is science which has produced and perpetuated human civilization. The process of science and development of human civilization have run parallel. Science has been a potent factor to shape the history of man's civilization on earth. Our forefathers lived in the jungles and we, now, are living in the atomic age. This long leap from the jungle to the atomic civilization could be possible only through science.

The concept of civilization is different from that of culture. Civilization includes the physical development while culture signuigies the inner growth. All the industrial, agricultural and technological developments are the essential parts of a developing civilization. We are not living in a world of dazzling glitter. Machines have reduced much of the human labour and suffering. They are serving humanity like faithful servants ours is a push button civilizations, which depends upon tools, impliments and machines.

There some specific features that make a civilization full. The entire structure of civilization stands some solid factors. The first condition for a true civilization is that is must include the fulfilment of the primary human necessities hust as fooding, clothing and housing. It is a matter of proud privilege that the present generation is enjoying better living conditions. We have better clothes to wear, better food to eat and a better house to live in than out ancestors. In this respect, we can assume an easy superiority over them. There is no denying the fact that it is science which has made our living conditions better. We have to be thankful to science for its myriad benedications.

The other factor which makes a civilization meaningful and useful is leisure. If a civilization can not provide leisure to the people, it is not a civilization of human being out of brutes. If a person is busy filling his belly from morning to evening, he does nothing different from what an animal does, and the person does not at all belong to a civilized society. The poor fellow struggle for his survival throughout his whole life and this is what the people of hunting and pastoral age, when there was no civilization, used to do.

Science has bestowed numerous gifts on mankind. Means of transport and communication, medical facilities, electricity, agricultural implements, recreational facilities etc. are such gifts of science to men. The blessings of science have made human life smooth and frictionless. It is a pity that the blessings of science have not benefited all the people equally as they have not reached all of them in fair measure. Our civilization is the civilization of only a few rich people equally as they have not reached all of them in fair measure. Our civilization is the civilization of only a few rich people. No civilization is complete unless it is shared commonly by all. Unfortunately the gulf between the rich and the poor has terribly widened at present. This has hampered the uniform development of our civilization.

Science has imprecated curses also no mankind. The destructive weapons of war have constantly been threatening the human civilization. The atomic weapons can destroy the human civilization in no time. Science can take away from us in a moment what it has given us during the last many ages.

The terror of war always hangs heavy upon our heads. The survival of humanity is facing a horrible peril. Thus, in this unclear are, the future of our civilization. Its quite unpredicatable. Science has made us unhappy by briging us a away from God and Nature. In this age of science, our life has become hectic and materialistic. How can there exist a true civilization in the midst of human sorrows and sufferings? If science has made the human civilization strong on one hand, it has made it weak on the other.

If the gifts of science are properly used and prudently harnessed, we can hope to bring about a lasting civilization which will become an abiding feature of human existence. Thus the wise use of science will strengthen the structure of civilization and make it perpetual. It can be safely concluded that science and civilization are inseparably related to each other.

SCIENCE AND AGRICULTURE

Science has revolutionised agriculture. It has helped in increasing production. With its help man has removed some natural hinderances. Agriculture is no longer dependent on rainfall or on climatic conditions. No doubt scientific research has not added any significant crop yet it has brought changes in methods employed in agriculture.

Agricultural production has increased many times because of science. It has given us fertilizers. In the past earth used to become deficient in salts and minerals. This was the cause of very low production. Now fertilisers provide these salts and minerals. Use of machines for ploughing and harvesting has helped in making maximum use of land.

Scientists have also given us new seeds which give better yield in shorter time. Irrigation is also mechanised. Plants can be protected against diseases and pests. Scientific methods are used for storing grains. Thus wastage is avoided.

Increase is agricultural production has changed the village life. The village economy has improved. The living conditions have become better. They are no longer backward. They are educated and publically conscious people.

In India application of science of agricultural is still to go a long way. Mechanisation of agriculture is not complete. In some states there is Green Revolution but other states are also to be covered. We can meet the growing demand for food only by applying science to agriculture.

LITERATURE AND SCIENCE

Literature and Science are two domains of learning which are by and large totally opposed to each other. However, a deeper consideration of both reveals a certain relation between science and literature.

Science is a search for truth and literature expresses that truth in a beautiful manner. For example, when science deflected the whole current of thought and Copernican theory (that the earth and other planets travel round the sun) became popular, Donne expressed it poetically.

"The new philosophy calls all in doubt,
The element of fire is quite put out,
The sun is lost, and the Earth and no man's wit,
Can well direct him where to look for it".

Another similarity is that the scientist looks at everything with the spirit of equiry and encourages keenness of the mind. Literature too needs a keenness of the mind to express the truths discovered by science.

Both science and literature are equally important in the development of a nation and its status in the world. Just as a country without scientific progress would be under developed, so too without a rich literature, a country would seem to have no soul. One can not imagine modern India without Aryabhatta, Homi Bhaba, C.V. Raman and others and neither can one imagine it without Tulsidas, Tagore, Premchand or R. K. Narayan. It is both the scientists and the literary artists right from ancient to the modern age which give any country its essential character.

The scientist is without sentiment. The scientific scholar may probe human nature but without a love for humanity. For instance, a botanist may be concerned only with the dissection of a flower and may never experience the charm and beauty of nature. The poet on the other hand, is carried away by the beauty of nature. Wordsworth's famous poem "The Daffodils" or "My heart leaps up, when I behold a rainbow in the sky" illustrates the joy of the artist in love with nature. The scientist would be more concerned with dissecting the colours of the rainbow and pointing out the scientific principle behind it.

Yet again, science sees man as a creature of the world—his thoughts and feelings to be understood by observation of his psychology and conclusions formed of his behaviour. Literature, however, sees man as a spiritual being, sees the beauty of living creatures, their emotions, thoughts and feelings are of concern not for psychological dissection, but to extol the essential goodness of man, and condemn the evil.

Thus, one can see essential similarities and immense differences between science and literature and the scientific temper of mind and the literary artists, temper of mind, and yet scientists have taken account of scientific discoveries in their works. The words of T.S. Eliot have been particularly affected by the spirit of science. In the poem "Wasteland" for exmaple, the entire poem is governed by the spirit of hollowness and frustration that has been brought about by scientific mechanization. H.G. Wells in his scientific romances such as "Time Machine", and "Invisible Man" has brought the imagination of an artist and poet. Issac Asimov in our time has written Science fiction showing how speculations of science for a world to come can be coloured by the imagination of an artist.

Thus, science and literature, though they appear to be poles apart, are yet related in various ways. Man is a complex creature, science was born from the insatiable curiosity of his intellect and science has flourished. But man is also a poetical creature and has expressed the wonders of science in his works. In the progress of both science and literature lies the greatness of every country.

SCIENCE AND RELIGION

Science and Religion, on the surface appear to be antithetical to each other, yet a closer look at the two reveals their interdependence on each other for a rational kind of life.

Now, science is based on rational thought. Scientists try to discover the reason behind natural phenomena. They follow the principle of cause and effect and give an explanation based on facts. Religion, however, tells us to accept many things without any question. Religion is based on faith, and not on rational thought. Thus, in method both science and religion are opposed to each other, yet both together have their importance for us in life.

If we look at science alone we can see the immense advantages that it has given us. Science has created modern civilization with its multistoryed buildings, swift means of transport on land, sea and air, life saving medicines and so on. However, science without exercising the guidelines laid down by religion, can do immense harm. Thus, while science has given us all the conveniences of modern life, it has also invented long range artillery guns, the atom bomb and the nuclear bomb. These inventions have already caused havoc in World War II. The principles laid down by religion are the only guidelines which can prevent man from using these engines of destruction for destructive purpose. Every religion teaches man to practise non-violence and respect the individuality and integrity of another human being. All religions also preach the virtue of forgiveness. Without a faith in these virtues preached by religion, man would lose his humanity and destroy the very civilization he has built.

Further, science does not teach us how to appreciate goodness and beauty. This very vital part of life is beyond its scope. Religion teaches us this. It teaches us to appreciate the beauty of a flower or a bird as much as the inner beauty residing in every man.

Yet religion without science is blind. It has tried to imprison truth in dogmas with often make people fanatics. This leads to religious wars in which the persons of different religions remain at longer heads trying to prove the superiority of their religion. It is here that scientific thought should be brought into play to show that all religious are the same; for scientific thought means to question and find out the truth, to question as to what all the fighting is about and come to a conclusion. Science encourages one to think while religion encourages one to believe.

Yet again, religion lays emphasis on rituals and ceremonies, the original meanings of which have been lost or are no longer relevant in our scientific age. Again, it is the task of scientific thought to point out the irrelevance of outdated customs in the modern scheme of things, and the value of retaining only those which are still relevant. Thus without exercising scientific thought one becomes narrow-minded and intolerant and blind to the needs to the times.

Yet again, religion discourages one from trying to find the unknown.

INDIAN ATOMIC ENERGY PROGRAMME

The Indian atomic energy programme has continuously benefitted from, and has in turn benefitted, the growth of the peaceful uses of nuclear energy in other countries. The numerous agreements signed by India with other countries for mutual co-operation and collaboration in various aspects of nuclear science and technology are testimony to our commitment to promote international understanding, and technoeconomic exchanges. On a bilateral basis and through the International Atomic Energy Agency exchange of experts and trainees in a host of specialized in seminar, conferences and symposia, have been the hall mark of our programme. Many trainees from other countries including a significant proportion from other developing countries have benefitted from the expertise and facilities available in our atomic energy establishments.

From the nature of scientific developments that have been taking place in the atomic energy programme, we have learnt some important lesson. Firstly, scientific, organization, where innovation is very important require different kinds of management and administrative systems. A very high degree of autonomy consistent with a high degree of accountability is necessary for scientific organization. Secondly, development of technology does not stop with research alone. In the Bhabha Atomic Research Centre we have combined the whole spectrum of activities in the transfer of technology continum. Its activities comprise design, development and production. There was a very high degree of self-reliance in fabricating equipment for research purposes, the scientists built up a very high degree of self-confidence to execute large programmes.

A whole range of electronic instruments for nuclear, industrial medical and scientific applications has been developed by the various units of the Department of Atomic Energy and has been successfully transferred to the Electronics Corporation of India. Efforts in laser technology have resulted in the development of instruments such as 'laser photocoagultor' for correcting retinal detachment. Gas chromatographic equipments indispensable for scientific research have been developed and licensed for manufacture by an Indian company.

The indigenous development and production of radio-pharmaceuticals and nuclear medical equipment such as 'scanners' have led to the utilization of advanced tools and techniques in the area of medical diagnosis and therapy for the welfare of the people. A major programme for increasing the coverage of nuclear medicine in the country from the present annual level of 0.07 by 1984—a ten-fold increase in ten years has been envisaged. For this purpose, four zonal radiation medicine centres, over a hundred small centres in the country's medical college, hospitals and a large radio-pharmaceuticals production plant are proposed to be set up.

A strong laedership, trust and support at the political level are essential for the success of such innovative programmes.

SHOULD INDIA MANUFACTURE NUCLEAR BOMB?

Some nations are exploiting the resources of Nature and developing the potentialities of human resources but others are manufacturing nuclear weapons. We talk of international co-operation and affirm the concept of international community but peace has been dodging us and war has all the time been threatening the world. So in .the light of these considerations, we will have to think whether India should manufacture nuclear weapons or not. We have been wedded to the policy of non-violence. Ardous effort for peace is the only sensible practical politics. We have been thinking of bringing order and raising human dignity to recreat a fine vision of the world.

Pakistan has always been trying to blackmail India. China has always been casting greedy eyes upon India. The Chinese had been training Nags and Mizos in order to create disruption in India.

In the present day world, there is a race for nuclear weapons. Every nation is trying its best, if it is within her capacity, to manufacture nuclear bombs. Naturally, if India manufactures these weapons, she will get high status among the community of nations. India has the potentiality to become the leader of Asia. But if we are not strong, from the military point of view, no nation is going to respect us.

It has been pointed out that India will have to incur a huge expenditure for manufacturing these weapons. Of course, it needs quite a big amount but can we afford to become weak militarily? Distance has been reduced and the nations have come closer, at least geographically, but the distance created by disagreement and difference still persists.

Under such circumstances even the smaller nations have started thinking of becoming nuclear powers. Nuclear weapons serve as damper for those nations which indulge in military adventures. American influence in Asia would fade away if India becomes an Asia leader. So India has no allies though many nations may show lip sympathy.

India's policy non-alignment which implies involvement in world politics without best raying any partially or prejudice has created uncertainty regarding India's affiliations. So we will have to depend upon our own resources for meeting the challenge of the enemies. China's nuclear explosion's have made us to feel that our neighbouring nations are having an edge over us. Nuclear weapons will give confidence and they will not bully us.

ATOMS IN PEASE AND WAR

An atom can be defined as the smallest particle into which anything can be broken down. For decades, scientist tried to find ways and means by which the energy inside each atom could be unlocked and put to work for mankind.

Within the last fifty years, scientists have learnt to release nuclear energy from the atoms of such minerals as uranium and plutonium. This nuclear energy thus released is also called atomic energy. Nuclear world is the greatest source for lighting, heating, operating factories, driving ships and countless other uses.

Nuclear power stations produce some of the electricity that people use everyday. Each station has a nuclear reactor in which nuclear fission takes place. Turbines powered by nuclear fission are also used to drive ships and submarines. Certain kinds of atoms produced during nuclear fission help doctors to diagnose disease, and to fight them. The atoms are called radio active isotopes. They also have many uses in industry and agriculture. Atomic energy is being used to meet the shortage of coal and petroleum in the world.

Atomic energy thus can be and is being used for positive purposes. However, people fear it, because it is also used to make bombs and other weapons that are the most terrible and destructive in the history of the world. The atom bomb used in the second world war to destroy Hiroshima and Nagasaki are examples of the havoc that can be wreaked by the misuse of atomic energy.

It is believed that the powerful nations such as the United States of America, the U.S.S.R. and even smaller nations have developed nuclear bombs which are powerful enough to destroy not merely a few cities in an explosion, but entire nations.

Less powerful bombs are used by various terrorist groups in various parts of the world to destalige the economy and fill fear in hearts in innocent peace poring people.

Thus, it is the hands man to use atoms and atomic energy for constructive or destructive purposes. It can be used to bring about progress and a better life for the people of the world or it can be used to terrorise the people and destroy mankind.

MY FAVOURITE SCIENTIST

My favourite scientist is Thomas Alva Edison. Now as a child he was considered to be a foll. He was not attentive to his studies and could not pull on well at school. His wise and sympathetic mother, however, succeeded in teaching him the essentials of education—reading, writing and arithmetic.

Pressed by poverty, Edison had to work for a living at an early age. But from his very childhood, he was fond of making various experiments some of which made him the laughing stock of the common people. A kind railway guard allowed him to set up his laboratory and printing press in compartment of the train. Besides selling fruits and candles, Edison sold his own newspaper edited and printed by himself. Unluckily one day a bottle broke and inflammable substance in it set fire to some of the boards. The angry guard put young Thomas along with his apparatus and printing press, out at the next station.

Edison now carried on his experiments at his home. One day he stood talking to a telegraph operator at the railway station when one of his children ran towards a coming train and jumped on to the lines. Edison dashed forward with the speed of lighting and brought the child out to safety as the train flashed by the operator, out of the gratitude, taught him telegraphy. Edison soon became an expert telegraph-operator.

Soon he got a golden opportunity. The Telegraphic Company of Newyork got into a fix. None of their engineers could remove a disorder in their system. Edison volunteered to find out the defect and soon set the system in operation. He was given a very handsome reward with which he set up a laboratory and factory of his own.

Edison had long dreams of seeing whole cities lighted with electricity. The arclights in use in his times was costly and could not be used on a large scale. He thought of a filament which could produce light when charged with electricity. He tried various materials but they were soon burnt out. He sent out men in search of a suitable substance and at last succeeded in obtaining a special type of cane for the purpose. The invention was perfected and today there is light not only in the street but in every house. Besides it is also very cheap.

The inventions of Edison are too numerous to be related here. Two of his remarkable inventions, however, need special mention. They are the gramophone and cinematography. After a long effort running into several years Edison succeeded in inventing photography. The principle underlying this is very simple. By means of an instrument the sound is beamed on a disc. A needle is then made to vibrate and with the help of a diaphragm the sound is reproduced.

One of the greatest contributions to the advancement of science is his work on cinematography. If the credit for this wonderful invention can go to one man, it is Edison.

People laughed at young Thomas Alva Edison when he tried to hatch an egg in imitation of the mother goose or made his friend swallow seidlitz power in the hope that this would produce a gas within the boy enabling him to fly. But the work done by him has not only astonished the world but also greatly benefited mankind. Edison died rich in money and fame. His untiring efforts were aimed at enriching the world with scientific knowledge and he succeeded even beyond his own expectations. So he is my favourite scientist.

IMPORTANCE OF ELECTRICITY

Ours is an age of science. Scientific inventions have made life easy and comfortable. The most useful of all the inventions is electricity. It is the master-key. It is always at our beck and caff. It serves us like a maid-servant.

Electricity has brought about a revolution in the life of man. It lights our houses and factories. We cannot do without electricity. The days of oil and gas lamps are a thing of the past. Even the bulbs are being replaced by flourescent and neon tubes. These tubes gives light that is quite harmless to the eyes. Instead, it has a soothing effect.

It is electricity that has make our life so comfortable. In summer, we do not feel the pinch of heat with the help of fans and room coolers. Some persons have got their rooms air-conditioned. Man rather enjoys life whether it is summer or cold. It is electricity which runs our refrigerators. We get cold water. We store vegetables an fruits that keep fresh in it. We enjoy cold drinks.

It is electricity which has made our life colourful and charming. The cinema houses run because of electricity. The film is projected and screened with the help of electricity. An evening spent in the cinema hall helps us forget the worries of the world. At home, our radio is operated with the help of electricity. The radio brings us only the voice but the television enables us to see the person also. Both the media give interesting and educational programmes.

More and more trains are now being run by electricity. These trains run at a very fast speed. These trains are therefore, becoming very popular.

Electricity plays an important role in the restoration of health. X-ray and ultra-scanning machines are operated with the help of electricity. The machines give clear and to the point diagonisis. Even operations cannot be performed without proper light.

Industry runs purely on electricity. No factory would work with it. Almost all machines work with the help of electricity.

The progress of agriculture also depends a lot on electricity. Fields are irrigated by tube-wells which are run by electricity.

Electricity is very useful in every sphere of our life. In the absence of electricity life becomes dull, boring and stagnant.

COMPUTERS

The progress of science has given us a large number of discoveries and inventions which have become the part and parcel of our life. The invention of computer may be regarded as the most wonderful achievement of modern science and progress. Now computers are very essential and popular in all departments.

The computer technology has changed fast from personal to mini, micro and super computer form. We can also quick and correct calculations, maintain heavy data and information and to a variety of other jobs by means of computers. It is an electronic means to receive, store and calculate data in the fastest way. A simple computer was first made by Charles Babbage in the 19th century. The computer age actually started in 1946 in the U.S.A.

There are different kinds of computers in the present-day world. They are vary according to their size, or memory (capacity). LAPTOP is the smallest computer today but CRAZ-2 is known to be the fastest computer. The personal and portable computers are used far and wide. IBM and APPLE-Inc are the biggest computer producing companies in the whole world. Hardware is its physical components and software is its set of instructions.

The practical usefulness of computers has been increasing by leaps and bounds both in India and the remaining part of the world. In India, the Tata Institute of Bombay produced the first computer in 1966 and its popularity has been gaining ground at a fast speed. the Bhabha Atomic Centre has helped much in its production. With the greater use of personal computers, there is a greater need of software pakages for more and more functions. Our students in schools and colleges get more and more information and knowledge in an effective way. Today they are widely used also in scientists, engineers, businessmen etc. everywhere.

Though we see a wide spread use of computers in banks, L.I.C. offices, schools, colleges, laboratories, libraries, etc. yet there is the want of trained computer operators. Truly twenty-first century shall be a computer dominated age.

MAN AND MACHINES

This is the age of machines. Man has become the slave of machines. He is too much dependent on machines. He wakes up with the help of an alarm clock. He shaves with the help of an electric shaver. Water for taking bath is supplied with the help of machines. There are machines which manufacture goods, machines which gives us extra-hands and extra power. Clearly machines have become our masters.

Machines have influenced our thinking and psychology. We have become mechanical in our behaviour. Milk of human kindness has become dry. We treat others not as human beings but as parts of an bigger machine called society. We do not love one another. A salesman will be happy to cheat a poor customer. A doctor would think of his fee more than the disease of the patient. Even the priests in the temple show greater respect to a rich person. So money and not human feelings guide us.

Machines have provided us sufficient spare time. So every one wants diversion during this time. Cheap entertainments have become popular. Drug addiction is one the increase. Boredom is the common disease of today.

Machines have made us time and speed conscious. Waiting even for a few minutes is troublesome. We seem to be running a hundred meter race. We are inventing the fastest means of communication and also destruction. This speed consiousness has given rise a number of dangerous diseases.

Despite the harm done by machines we cannot dispense with them. Imagine what may happen if all the mills factories are closed. How uncomfortable man will feel it there are no means of communication. Machines have become a part of human life.

TELEVISION AND ITS VALUE

"Television is one of the most wonderful and latest gift of science to man for his profit and pleasure."

The world of today in which we live is quite different from the world of yesterday. It is because of science, on which the modern life is based. Science has come with Aladdin's lamp in its hand to help man with various gifts. In fact science is a boon and it has done wonders in every walk of man's life. There are hundreds of gifts of science which have made man's life easier, better and happier.

Television is a wonderful gift. With its help a man is able not only to hear voice but also to see the faces of persons acting, singing or talking thousands of kilometers away. The credit for the mirculous inventions of television goes to Mr. John L. Baird, a scientist of Scotland. Television is an improvement on the wireless of Marconi. In short, television is a magic-box which installed in a room, makes it a cinema hall. Man sists leisturely and enjoys various programmes appearing on the screen.

Initially, television gave black and white impressions. Now colour television has become popular. Television was first introduced on an exprimental basis in Delhi (India) in 1959. By that time, many western countries had already changed over from black and white to colour T.V. Today in India also there is a craze for colour T.V. It has become a symbol of status. Colour television is far more successful in making programmes interesting, impressive and effective, because people have a natural liking for colours.

Television is a greatly source of recreation, entertainment and pastime. We sit comfortably in our room and enjoy various programmes presented on the screen—dramas, stories, music, dance, etc. and for some time we forget worries and boredom of life and feel fresh.

Further, television plays a great role in informing and educating the masses about family planning, health, sanitation, nutrition, agriculture, etc. Besides, television is a good means of advertisement and propaganda also.

Television has great potential as an instrument of education. Education through television seeks to resolve three problems :

(a) Over-crowding in schools,

(b) Shortage of laboratory space and equipment,

(c) Lack of adequate number of trained science teachers. The television programmes are syllabus-based and are integrated in the school time-table.

Education through television in India beginning 1959 as a social education project. It was aimed at the middle and higher secondary school, run by the Delhi administration. Since then it has become popular.

Today television is a useful aid to teaching. Students see more and better experiments on the screen. Some of the experiments shown on television are such that even other best schools could not provide.

Television promises bright future. As an instrument for education it is very popular in America but the day is not far when it will be so in India also. Television has made living better and added lustre to life. However, nothing should be done in excess. Over exposure of children to television is injurious to their eyes and to their studies.

INDIAN EDUCATION

THE NEW PATTERN OF EDUCATION : 10 + 2 + 3

It was Lord Macaulay, an English Educationist who started the present system of education in India. It has been continuing here since without much significant change and improvement. His aim was to get an army of English-knowing clerks from the country. In free India, that system does not apply well to our social and human needs.

The system of new pattern of education (10 + 2 + 3) was introduced in some states of the country on the recommendations of an Education Commission which was appointed by the Government. Though some states have been practising the new pattern of education since 1975, yet needed desirable (useful) results have not been so far achieved (got). This system was also adopted on the advice of the Central Board of Education.

According to this system, a student could become a graduate in 15 years instead of 14 years. Much emphasis is laid (put) under the new system on vocational education. If a student does not show brilliant results, he should give up education and start some vocation (work) of his own. For this, it is compulsory to give vocational education, or training to all students at least for an hour daily. This system of education has been joining on Delhi and some other states.

The silver-lining (advantage) of this system is that students get an opportunity (change) to learn an art, or occupation to earn their bread and butter (livelihood) in their future life. The number of students under this system is increasing but its utility (usefulness) is far from satisfactory. The Ex-Prime Minister of India, Sri Morarji Desai opposed it saying it as an extra burden to our students.

If we sit to analyse the new system of education. We find several short-comings :

First of all, there is the want of trained and experienced teachers for teaching and training the students in different crafts.

Secondly, there is the need of funds for starting well-equipped workshops for such vocational education and training.

Thirdly, the private managements of schools in Delhi and some other states do not show any interest in making at successful.

Lastly, there is no needed help and financial aid from Central and State Governments.

The above discussion clearly shows that this system is not useful and practical to all students in the country. It may prove useful only to selected brilliant students. In this way, a better and more practical system of education is the need of the hour. It can evolved only with the close cooperation both of State Government and Central Government.

EXAMINATIONS

Students look upon examinations with contempt; they make all possible effort to avoid them. Educationists are against them and are thinking of abolishing them. Critics find falt with them. Inspite of condemnation from all quarters, examinations persist. They seem indispensable in every walk of life. They are like milestone on the road to education and life.

Examinations are not necessarily the sure test of the ability of students. They are judges from what they perform in the exams. Sometimes the most brilliant students is not able to do justice in such a short duration. On the contray a student who has not touched the books the whole year gets good marks because all the questions he prepared just before the examination were asked.

Shakespeare never passed any examination yet his works have won world-wide recognition. The world's greatest scientist Einstein, father of the atomic age failed in Mathematics. Mahatma Gandhi and Pandit Nehru were not record-breakers at the university though their personalities shook the whole world. Examinations do determine the value of majority of the students, but the geniuses have often proved misfit at the examinations.

With all the faults, examinations are an incentive to hard work. They are indeed a necessity because it is only the fear of the examination that makes students work hard. Examinations are a necessary evil. It is not possible to do without them. They will remain in one form or the other. After all, this life is a long examination and we have to take it.

CO-EDUCATION

Co-education is the outcome of a general movement for the emancipation of women and the declaration of their rights and eligibility to all kinds of social activities and awareness of employment.

Co-education is economical and is specially suited for a poor country like India. Moreover, co-education enables boys and girls to come into contact with one another. An environment, for the purpose of a complete education cannot exclude the relation between the sexes.

Co-education paves the way for the operation of wholesome influence which one sex exercise on the other. Co-education produces a healthy spirit of competition between boys and girls, and leads to greater efficiency. The brilliant results shown by institutions where boys and girls study together bear testimony to it.

Co-education, however, is not an unmixed blessing. Stephen Leacock, in his essay, has expressed himself against co-education—not that co-education is morally undesirable, but that it is incomplete with serious study.

There are some others who think that free mixing of boys and girls leads to romance and sentimentalism and they try to translate into their life stories of the films. Thus mixing of sexes at the adolescent stage when sex urge is at highest pitch is not advisable.

Recently a church of England clergymen has attributed the loose morals of American youth to the system of co-education.

The same curriculum does not suit both sexes; as there are wide differences between their mental constitutions. Dr. Joad had remarked; Girls tend to be more interested in their immediate surrounding in what is pretty and ornamental; boys in what is more remote from them, in what is useful, in what is general. Boys seeks expression in investigating exploring, constructing. Girls through artistic and emotional changes.

The right to study with men in the same institutions cannot be denied to women whether it is beneficial or harmful.

VALUE OF BOOKS

Books are the store house of information, knowledge and wisdom. In the words of Milton "a good book is the life-blood of a master spirit, embalmed and treasured upon purpose to a life beyond life. They give us company in solitude. They are our never-failing friends."

In the words of Bacon, "they serve for delight, for ornament and for ability. They offer us opportunities for a welcome escape from the monotony of routine life."

Reading maketh a full man, conference a ready man and writing an exact man. Some books are to be tasted, others to be swallowed and some few are to chewed and digested. They add knowledge, expand our mental horizon and make us wiser and happier.

In the words of Louis Stevenson, books are a mighty bloodless substitute for life. He has condemned books the study of which, he thinks, is the weariness of flesh. But if books are completely neglected it result in the barrenness of mind and makes us ignorant, orthodox and superstitious. So the complete neglect of books is as undesirable as too much study of books. The market is flooded with all sort of books. We should make a judicious selection of them.

MY FAVOURITE TEACHER

I read in class XI. From class VI, I have been studying in this very school. Mr. H.C. Sharma is my favourite teacher. I am acquainted with his habits and behaviour for the last six years.

He is an M.A. M.C.I.E. Besides being my class teacher, he teaches us English. He is very experienced and teaches us very well. He is the master of his subject. He knows the art of teaching well. He makes his lessons very interesting. He puts life in his presentation. He treats his students like his children. When a student comits a mistake, he makes him realise it tactfully. He is never cross with them. He believes in simple living and high thinking.

He never sets a wrong example before his students. He has a spotless character. He takes interest in extra-curricular activities and games. He is very strict about discipline. He always comes in time and expects that his students too should develop the same habit.

He practices in his own life what he preaches to his students. He is a true friend, Philosopher and guide to his students.

On account of his qualities, Shri Sharma has become a very popular teacher in our school and hence he is my favourite teacher.

OUR SCHOOL PEON

There are ten peons in my school. Suresh is one of them. He is about 50 years old. He is lean and thin. He wears a Khaki shirt and Khaki trousers. He wears a cap on his head.

His duties are not many. He generally sits on the bench outside the Principal's Office. He attends to the calls of the Principal. He does not allow any visitor to enter the Principal's Office without permission.

Suresh is the oldest peon in the school. He is very honest and sincere. The Principal has full faith in him. He sometimes transacts money to the bank. He is very humble and polite. He obeys the orders of the teachers and the office clerks.

He is head peon. He thinks himself to be the master of other peons and often scolds them. He makes them to work.

Suresh never gets angry with the students. He loves them as his young ones. He helps them in their need. But he does not allow any student to make mischief. All the students fear him very much.

I like Suresh very much. He is very low paid but he looks after a big family. He lives hand to mouth. I sometimes offer him some money on festival days and give him old clothes for his children to wear.

TRAVELLING—A PART OF EDUCATION

Travelling for the young is a part of education. Life is real, life is practical but much of what a man learns from books is theoretical. Therefore, he is required to have practical knowledge of men and things. This practical knowledge is gathered from the first hand knowledge of outside world.

The more a man travels, the more he sees of the world. A young man who has never set foot out of his home grows a narrow outlook.

Travelling does not only give us a better understanding of other people but at the same time it enables us to have an impartial and detached view of our own accomplishment.

Travelling encourages a sense of enterprise, action and adventure. History is full of such instances where ignorant and timid people have been subjected to domination by enterprising and daring nations.

Travelling is a source of joy and pleasure. Today science has made travelling easy, swift and comfortable.

Travelling teaches us the value of sociability and good manners. We grow tolerant, modest and self-assertive. The free intercourse with other people tends to make us broad-minded, accommodating and truly intelligent.

However, in order that we may profit by travel, we must travel with open eyes, open mind and a sympathetic heart. It is essential that we must possess charity and courtesy. We must not only travel for the sale of pleasure but with a desire to see, learn and understand. It is true that no education is complete without travelling.

A LITTLE KNOWLEDGE IS A DANGEROUS THING

Knowledge is desirable, and should be attained at any cost, but a little knowledge though certainly better than no knowledge, has the dangerous tendency of turning the head of its owner.

There is certainly a great deal of truth in the statement. It is quite common to see persons will shallow attainments parading their knowledge. This leads them to treat others with scant respect. They want that others should respect and admire them all fairly makes them unpopular, if not hateful.

"An empty vessel makes much noise". A man with a little knowledge or skill in medicine or surgery may kill his patients. A novice driving a car or bus may put lives of his passengers to an end. The scientists who invent nuclear war heads are wanting in religious and moral education. The quack who plays with lives of poor patients is himself victim of imperfect knowledge.

True knowledge is a power. The poet, Pope, therefore, advises us to drink deep at the fountain of knowledge. A little knowledge is not a dangerous thing in itself. But the vanity, it brings and the desire to show off oneself realy is dangerous.

THE PROBLEM OF STUDENT'S INDISCIPLINE

The youths of today are the leaders of tomorrow. The students are the backbone of our nation. On their useful effects depend our social uplift and national progress. With this reason, it is very necessary that they should play their active and useful role.

It is a very serious social as well as national problems that we often hear of student's indiscipline. They cut their classes, go on general strike and even destroy national property. In free India, there is wide spread unrest among students far and wide in the country.

It is a very sad state of affairs when we hear that academic sessions start late, their examinations are held in the months of June and July and the results are declared in November and December. Thus the youth energy goes waste and national progress is hundred (checked). No society, or courtry can made necessary progress without students discipline which is much needed.

The main causes of indiscipline among students are briefly discussed into the following lines :

(1) The present system of education is out of date. It is neither useful to our social needs, nor it trains students to earn the living in future.

(2) The present system of examinations is fully theoretical and develop mass-copying.
Throughout the year, students remain idle, so an empty mind is only devil's workshop.

(3) No moral education is given to students whose character-building remains only a dream.

(4) The problem of unemployment gives rise to indiscipline and even criminal acts among our students in the country.

In view of the above causes of indiscipline among students some remedies, or suggestions for the solution of this burning problem are given in the following lines :

First of all, the present of education should be made according to our social needs. Their education should teach and train them to earn their bread and butter in their future life. For this, vocational and technical education should be given to more and more students.

Secondly, the present to examinations which has become out-of-date should be changed and improved to make it real, practical and useful 'Cramming' and 'copying' should be discouraged at all level.

Thirdly, qualified and devoted teachers should be appointed. Then they will inspire their students for a discipline life and useful activity for our society and the country.

Lastly, our students be kept free from the evil effect of political parties who use them as their instrument for their own advantages. They often instigate them for the indisciplined and violent acts and even include them in general strikes and market closures, etc.

Students who are the pillars of our nation should be trained as useful citizens of the country. India is a developing nation where they should play their active and useful role in nation-building. Only then we may hope for real and greater progress in the country.

KNOWLEDGE IS POWER

Man has great love for power. He has been trying to influence others in various ways. For gaining power he took the help of religion, supporters or government. Religious priests enjoy huge powers even today. Political leaders employ all methods to remain in power. Another source of power now a days is knowledge.

Knowledge of the working of the minds of human beings gives power over others. By using psychological methods human beings are made slaves. Russian people were made to believe in communism. Hitler stuffed the minds of the people with his ideas. Religious purohits also make the people to believe in a particular philosophy. With the help of knowledge people are made slaves.

Knowledge of a business makes the person to have an upper hand. If you take to a work which you do not know you fail. Knowledge of work will make you superior to other workers. You can manage it properly.

If a doctor has a complete knowledge of his profession he commands respect. Such a doctor will have confidence. Knowledge will give him power over other.

If a political leaders understands the problems of people he can rule others. He should feel the pulse of the people. He should give what others want. He sould be able to exploit the weakness of the people. Knowledge of the economic conditions of the people will give him a shot in the arm.

Knowledge of the self is perhaps the greatest weapon one can have. If you know yourself you can do many things which others cannot do. You can conduct yourself in a better manner.

So knowledge whether of subjects or of affairs or self gives extra power to handle things. If may take time to acquire knowledge but once acquired it gives us extra hands and extra means.

OUR NATIONAL IDENTITIES

MY COUNTRY

India, the biggest democracy and one of the oldest civilizations of the world, is the second most populated country in the world after China. India is my country. It is a country of villages. Most people live in the villages than in the cities. There are big cities like Bombay and Delhi. It is a free country now. Before 1947, it was ruled by the British.

The Himalayas, the highest mountain in the world, are in the north. The Indian Ocean is in the south. There are many rivers but the Ganga is the longest. It is a sacred river in India. We have set up big industries and built dams. We grow several kinds of crops too.

India is known for its lions, elephants and tiger. The peacock is the national bird of India. There are many forests, lakes and valleys. It is a country of great saints and sages. She has given birth to scholars like C.V. Raman, Ravinder Nath Tagore, Dr. J.C. Bose and Dr. Homi Bhabha.

The land of Upnishads, the Mahabharata, and the Ramayana has been the cradle of ancient civilization. Under the British oppression, her spirit was suppressed. Leaders like Mahatma Gandhi, Subhash Chandra Bose, Sardar Patal got her freedom. Since then our country has been making steady progress in the field of agriculture, education, medicine, science and industry. Today, we are self-sufficient in almost every sphere of life.

NATIONAL FLAG

Evey country has its own national flag. Till 15th August, 1947, we were under the British Rule and were not free. The Union Jack, the National Flag of England, flew all over India. We got independence on August 15, 1947 and our National Flag replaced the Union Jack. The National Flag is a symbol of our sovereignty. There may be many political parties in a country like ours and each party may have its own flag. But all citizens and all parties show obedience and loyalty to the National Flag. It is the symbol of the sovereign Government.

The need for a National Flag for free India was thought of as early as on June 3, 1947 by the British Government and a committee was constituted to suggest a National Flag acceptable to all parties. The committee constituted for the purpose made the following recommendations :

(1) The flag should be tricoloured with three bands horizontally arranged.

(2) The flag of the Indian National Congress be adopted as the National Flag of India with suitable modifications to make it acceptable to all parties and communities in India.

(3) The colour of the emblem should be dark blue.

(4) The colours should be in the following order, Saffron at the top, white in the middle, and dark green at the bottom.

(5) The emblem of the flag should be an extact reproduction of the wheel, the capital of Ashoka

Sarnath Pillar, superimposed in the middle of the white band.

On July 22, 1947 the specimen of the National Flag was placed before members of the Constituent Assembly was placed before members of the Constituent Assembly for their approval, with some more suggestions, *i.e.* The colour of the wheel shall be navy blue, and the designs to be as on the abacus of the Sarnath Lions Capital of Ashoka. The diameter of the wheel shall be approximate to the width of the white band. The ratio of the width to the length of the flag shall be 2 width to 3 breaths.

The flag was adopted by the Constituent Assembly. Smt. Hamsa Mehta presented the new National Flag to Rajendra Prasad who was the President of the Constituent Assembly. On August 15, the National Flag went up on the Viceregal lodge with 31 gun salute. India's National Flag replaced the Union Jack on the central secretariat. The first public salutation for the National Flag was conducted on the evening of 15th August, 1947. On August 16th at 8.30 a.m. in 1947 Pandit Jawaharlal Nehru hoisted the national flag for the first time on the ramparts of the Redfort in Delhi.

The design for this National Flag was drawn by Sri Venkaiah of Andhra Pradesh. The significance of the flag and its colours are :

(1) Saffron stands for renunciation.

(2) White stands for truth and purity, and

(3) Green for plant life on which our very life exists. Wheel stands for motion.

There are set designs for National Flag :

(1) 6" × 4".

(2) 9" × 6".

(3) 21" × 14".

(4) 9" × 6".

(5) 12" × 8".

(6) 6" × 4".

(7) 18" × 12".

(8) 3" × 2".

The ratio between the length and the breadth of the Indian National Flag is 3 : 2. The Flag should be hoisted and lowered briskly. The Flag should be flown sunrise to sunset. There are certain Don'ts about the use of National Flag :

(1) It should not be flown with Saffron colour down.

(2) It shall not be allowed to touch the ground, flow or trail in water.

(3) It should not be used as a drapery in any form except on occasions specified.

The use of National Flag are usually permitted on all Government buildings, courts and on cars of specified dignitaries. On certain occasions like Republic Day, Independence Day, Mahatma Gandhi's Birthday.

When the state mourning is declared, National Flag is flown half mast. National Anthem is sung after the flag is hoisted and a salute given. In school Pledges are taken as stated as under :

"I pledge allegiance to the National Flag and to the Sovereign Democratic Republic for which it stands."

Whenever our President or Prime Minister visits the other countries there also our National Flag is flown along with other National Flag.

NATIONAL INTEGRATION

Today, we stand divided almost on every point our unity stands shattered. Vested interests, sectional views mutual suspicious, reactionary elements, both communal and linguistic, reap rich harvest in the midst of economic exigencies, gigantic population problem soaring princes and numerous other formidable problems threaten the very survival and the bare existence of the masses.

Indeed, the greatest task before us is the building up of the unity and solidarity of our people. Our country has often stood as a solid rock in face of common danger such as armed conflict with Pakistan.

In simplest words, national integration means a warm hearted love and sympathy of one Indian for every other. It is for that reason all the people belonging to different parts of the country, however strong their feeling might be on particular issues must never forget that they are Indian first. National Integration means the revival of the lost sense of responsibility towards country, re-affirmation of our faith in democratic way of life, rededication to nation building activities. Only the maximum happiness of the maximum number of people means true freedom and also true progress.

We must understand the nation. Today we think with our stomach, see with our nakedness and feel with our misery.

It is a pity that though India is a secular country, the religious differences yet lead to violent clashes. Secularism which means tolerance to all belief still leads to rivalries and conflicts often taken the shape of exhibiting the importance and prestige of one religion over the other. The question of high and low castes and scheduled tribes continues to suffer neglect and endure disabilities. Provincialism is worst enemy of national unification and linguistic agitation has led the youth to indulge in indiscriminate acts of rowdyism.

Besides, various political parties must grow out of their politics and lend a helping hand in the task of building a nation. The enlightened view to our differences can make us realise that we are all different elements working in different ways towards a common goal-prosperity and welfare of our country that is India.

INDIA'S CULTURE

"Culture is the expression of our nature in our modes of living, and of thinking, in our everyday intercourse, in art, in literature, in religion, in recreation and enjoyment."

—MacIlver

Culture is the total way of life of a person on their experiences and tests of different times. India's culture has a very old and huge history. It has seen many ups and downs and has survived. The cause of its survival is its own high elements. Foreign invasions, the naked sword of curuel Aurangzeb, the tyranny of Nadir Shah and the sugar-coated pills of western culture and civilization could not harm it even in the least. Various attempts of running it and ups and downs have made it more strong and rich. Like gold, it has got its intrinsic value which never suffers a loss and like the Polar Star it is shining in the world.

India's culture is highest in degree, riches in store, oldest in time and continued in existence. The ancient cultures of other countries have died and are now a thing of story, history and imagination. But India is fortunate; its ancient culture is still continued and is at present fully alive and active on sacred land. Greece, Rome, Egypt and China are not today what they were yesterday. But India is same today as it was yesterday, and it will be same in the times to come. In other words, India was India yesterday, it is India today and it will be India tomorrow.

India's culture is deep-rooted and highly developed. On its basis it has secured a place of pride and distinction on the earth. It is based on universal and everlasting values of life. It is piercing out of the deep dark ravines of the haory past and is giving proof of its continued existence and excellence and it is blossoming like a pretty flower. Many a thousand year old ways of living, ideas, rules of conduct, social organisations, various religious beliefs and practices, system of government etc., are seen in India even today is some or the other form. In a word, the pattern of Indian life and ideals has remained same through the long process of time.

As regards the elements of India's culture, the first is the mediation between God and Man. Man is the highest creation of God. In India people have realised it always and have tried to have a communion with God through mediation, prayer and worshipping, They have a constant aspiration for their creator. The second is religious attitude; India's culture has been ever associated with religion. We see that religious motive is predominent in poetry, drama, architecture, music and dance. In perhaps no other country is religion so truly the heart and soul of culture. Dominence of religion has turned the whole Indian life into sacrament.

The third is spritualism. India has always made efforts to seek and serve the divinity within and insisted on balance and order which give sobriety to the ways of life. Our forefathers has no hunger material goods. They looked upon the world as an illusion, and did not care much for material gains and considerations. The fourth is belief in co-existence. India has ever believed in the policy of 'Live and let live. The fifth is belief in international brotherhood; India has always belonged to the humanity more than to nationality. The sixth is non-violence in conduct; Gautama Buddha, Mahavir Swami and Gandhiji are good examples in this respect.

The seventh is the high status of woman. In India woman has been regarded as an object of worship and adoration and she has been called the 'Lakshmi' of the house. Gods reside in the house where the woman is adored. History shows that in the whole world woman has not secured such prestige, honour and regard as on the divine land of India. Lord Ram had to set up and place a statue of gold of Sita in order to organise and perform 'Ashwamedh Yaga'.

The eight is the graded social structure. In order to make the society run smoothly and efficiently, our forefathers had stratification of the society. They divided the whole society into four classes known as four castes and assigned different duties to each section.

The ninth is marking life stages. In order to make the journey of human life in the world a real success, our forefathers marked human life into four stages known as four 'Ashrams'.

The tenth is plain living and high thinking. It is the guiding principles of India's life. The dress of Indians is generally simple and they have always tried to restrict their needs to the minimum. They are noted for their high ideas relating to rules of good conduct and morality and notions of charity, hospitality and neighbourliness.

The eleventh is great esteem for education and fine arts. Teachers and artists commanded great respect in our ancient society. The twelfth is agricultural economy. India is an agricultural country. Its population in majority live in villages. In olden times each village was self-sufficient.

FUTURE OF DEMOCRACY IN INDIA

People express their genuine doubts about the future of democracy in India. Obviously their view is that Indian democracy is at cross roads. Even educated and informed people feel that our democracy is disintegrating and those who had complete faith in its success also feel disillusioned. However, we must realise that while country is passing through a rough phase, there is no cause to feel unduly despondent.

There is only doubt that Indian scene today presents a discordant scene. There are endless controversies on almost every question. Indeed, deterioration in law and order is the most painful.

Lack of direction, purposelessness, hesitancy and indecisiveness have shaken the faith of the people. However, we must realise that these by themselves cannot be attributed as the defects of democracy. They are not endemic to a system. Any society whatever its political compulsion has its own phases of sluggishness and buoyancy.

Opportunism flourishes, convictions occupy a secondary importance. Ideology has come to be identified with exigency. Everybody seems to be for himself. Mostly group combinations with nothing common between them, but he consuming love of power, are ruling the roost in many places. It is on the basis of such a state of affairs that people sadly admit that democracy has failed both as a system of Government and as a way of life.

However, we must realise that it is only a passing phrase. The same and even worse had happened in other countries. All the political parties.

Convulsions are essential because then alone more viable aggregates of political power shall emerge.

Democracy is essentially a doctrine of 'protest'. Therefore, even when people are divided on most details, they are united. The fact is that the Indian society is in the thores of a change. As such, the only remedy is increased production and accurate economic activity preceded by better distribution.

However, we must understand that democracy is not an end in itself buy only a means to the end. There is no royal road to development. Development is an exacting process which demands its price. We must learn that the democracy enjoins the opportunity and burden of choice. Democracy and responsibility are inseparable. Faith and hope are also the essential parts of democracy.

We do not claim that democracy is a flawless system, but it is also not a cut and dried formula which people can adopt and put it to practice without training. Democracy is a way of life. Which has to be solved and profited by rigorous and conscientious efforts. It is essential that the individual is enlightened, responsible and vigilant. We have the eyes of the world focussed on us. This colossal experimentation must succeed if the people in this continent have to survive.

FORESTS FOR NATIONAL WELFARE

Trees are amongst man's most reliable friends and a country which cares for its future must take good care of its forests. It is human greed which a responsible for the destruction of forests and this has caused a great ecological damage. Forests can survive only if forestry is attuned to the goal of the national development.

New forests should be planted and where there is space in old forestry. Rural people need wood for the production of domestic fuel and raw material for industries like paper, pulp, plywood etc. The simultaneous increase in demand for food crops like tea, suffer etc., towns hips, roadways, hydroelectric projects, make it difficult to extend forests. But without having proper balance human life will be in danger because ecological imbalance affect the living conditions as well as the life of living creatures.

Forests are renewable sources of energy. We must pan so that forests can co-exit with and enlarge side by side with the growth of agriculture and industries. Forests not only beautify the environment they give us many things which are necessary for the existence of the human being.

Forestry development programmes lay special emphasis on raising man made forests to meet the long-term requirements of various forest products. The measures to augment full wood resources and small wood for farmers through social forestry schemes have also been initiated. Side by side, new planting programmes have been taken up in the states and Union Territories to increase the forests wealth in the country.

The National Commission on Agriculture strongly has recommended the establishment of Forest Development Corporations in the States and Union Territories to arrange institutional finance for the development of forests in our country.

AN ELECTION SCENE

In a democratic country, elected representatives run the government. India is a democratic country. So elections, are held from time to time. Elections are held for Parliament and the State Assemblies.

In November 1992, the elections for the Parliament were held in India. Main political parties such as Congress, Janta Dal, B.J.P., Communist party fought the elections. Some of the candidates fought as independents.

About three weeks before the election, canvassing started. The candidates and their supporters went from door to door in their constituencies to seek votes. Leaflets and hand bills were distributed among the people and stuck on walls. Meetings were held and speeches were delivered. The leader and supporters of political parties addressed large gatherings. They put before the public the programme of their parties. They appealed to the voters to vote for their candidates. Loudspeakers were fully used.

At last the election day came. Twenty four hours, before the election, the canvassing stopped. All offices and institutions were closed on that day. I was not a voter but I went to see how voting took place. My college was also a polling station. So, I went there to see the polling.

I saw a few tents put up near polling booth. They belonged to different parties. Each had engaged rickshaw, tongas and other vehicles to carry the voters. Voters began to arrive there. Some policeman were posted there to maintain law and order.

The voting started at 8 a.m. It was a very simple process. The voter was given a ballot paper. The voter's finger was marked with indelible ink so that he or she might not vote twice. The voter went behind a curtain where ballot boxes were placed on a table. He put cross mark on a ballot paper against the name of the candidate for whom he or she wanted to vote. Then the voter dropped it into the ballot box.

When the polling was over, the ballot boxes were properly sealed and sent to counting station. Thus polling came to an end.

It was a delightful scene. People came by different vehicles. Women came in groups singing. For them, it was some religious ceremony.

A GOOD CITIZEN

Man is a social animal. There can be no citizen without a state. As the subject of a state every citizen has some duties and he enjoys at state time certain rights. Some times he has to put up with some inconveniences and at other he enjoys many special benefits all for the good of the country to which he belongs. He has a right to take part in the legislative as well as judicial activities of that state and can give full expression to his views and opinions from the platform and through the Press. But he has responsibilities also. He must protect the weak against the strong and stand always by the state.

A good citizen, therefore, is one who is always loyal and faithful to his country and like a true patriot is prepared to sacrifice his all for the good of the land of his birth. He is ready even to shed his blood for the honour and glory of his country.

A good citizen is not a mere law abiding person but one who has the good of his country at heart. He must respect the traditions of his country and at the same time strive for reform. To raise his country to a higher level of civilization must be his aim. A good citizen is one who has deep respect for the past of his country striving for a greater future for his country. He must not forget that the future, no less than the present, is always lines with the past.

A good citizen must live at peace with his fellow citizens, respecting the laws of the state. He should have love for the institutions of his country and help the state against criminals and law breakes at times of need. He should exert his influence to bring about reforms in the state, if reforms are needed, and should not be blindly conservative. He should understand the existing educational and other institutions of the land and make efforts to bring about desirable improvements.

A good citizen must be kind, sympathetic and soothing to his fellow-beings. He must respect the rights and privileges of others and should be only as he wished to be done by. He must feel himself a member of the organisation—a small part of a big whole and realise that his actions, thoughts and deeds will contribute to the making or the pooling of the whole to which he belongs. He must, therefore, subordinate his personal interests to the higher good of the state, selflessness, selfsacrifice and consideration for the greatest good of the greatest number should be the guiding principles of his life and conduct.

INDIA'S NATIONAL EMBLEM

National Emblem is one of the three tnings which every free country has for its representation, the other two being

The Chakra stands for motion, dynamism and progress. It gives us the message that we should move forward always and should not stop. The words; 'Satyameva Jayate' mean 'Truth alone Triumphs'. These embody a cardinal principle of our way of life to see Truth and be guided by Truth.

Thus in totality, the Emblem stands for strength, righteousness, justice, truth and fair-play.

CONQUESTS OF PEACE ARE GREATER THAN THOSE OF WAR

War wastes a nation's wealth. War promotes cruelty, kills the noble instinct of man. If one gains in patriotism, one loses in truth, kindness, tolerance and honesty.

Peace brings happiness, prosperity and contentment. The victories of peace have been won over the forces of hatred, over disease, over pain and suffering, over poverty and ignorance over great political and social wrongs. The fact remains that all these things which lie at the foundation of human literature, art and architecture, trade and commerce, and education can flourish in times of peace only. It is rightly said, "Peace is breath of God, war is the drone of devil".

War results in loss of life to the victors and vanquished alike. Mass slaughter of mankind brings a slur and shame on the fair name of human civilization. Trade, Industry, Commerce and Agriculture are paralysed. Victories of war attract attention far more rapidly than the calm and quiet achievement of peace. It is really strange in war we aspire for peace and in peace prepare for war.

When peace reigns supreme, the mind of man turns towards constructive values of life. Peace substitutes hatred with love, revenge with forgiveness and death with life.

It is a strange paradox that even aim of war is peace. Nations go to war because they with to achieve. The weapons of Mahatma Gandhi were not the deadly weapons of war but weapons of truth and non-violence.

Cicero spoke the truth, "I prefer the most unjust peace to a just war that will evil waged".

It is only during peace that a literacy campaign can be started that standard of living of masses can be raised, that better houses can be built for poor, that more schools and colleges, can be opened, that persons can be reformed, that crime can be effectively checked.

MY VILLAGE

The name of my village is Maukhas. It is situated on Pucca road which leads to Garh. It is on the border line of Calcutta. There is a big pond near my village.

My village is quite big. There are about 1,900 houses in my village. Its population is about 30,000. The chief occupation is agriculture. Morning and evening, people are always busy in fields, preparing the lands, manuring it, feeding the cattle and harvesting. Some of them take weaving and spinning. Some are engaged in cottage industries.

Some of the houses are pucca but most of the houses are built of mud. There is an Intermediate College and a Junior High School in the village. The villagers have love for education. But a very few boys read there. Instead of reading, they work in their fields. There is also a post office in my village.

My people lead a simple and happy life. They enjoy a good health. Real life is there in them. They are honest. My village is making progress. I like it. I pray to God to give them moral courage so that they may lead a happy life.

OUR LIFE AND ITS VALUES

THE AIM OF YOUR LIFE

Every young man has an aim or ambition in life. A man without an aim cannot succeed. He cannot achieve his goal. In fact, it is an aim, that makes a man active. Without aim a man civilization is one of man's aims and his efforts to achieve them.

The aim of my life is to become a doctor. There is a reason why I have chosen this career. Once one of my classmates fell it. As he was poor, he could not get proper medical aid. His condition grew worse day by day. When I went so see him, he looked at me helplessly. After a few days of illness, he died. It gave me a terrible shock. I began to think about the suffering of people. I decided to become a doctor and do some service to the sick people.

I will study hard to qualify myself as a doctor. When I become a qualified doctor I will move to the country side and set up a dispensary there. I am sorry to say that doctors wish to live in cities. They do not feel that their need in villages is greater. But I would like to serve villages. I will work day and night to serve people. I will keep in mind that people need consolation and sympathy more than medicine.

I will not be money-minded. I find that doctors have lost reputation because they are money-minded. They have brought bad name to this noble profession. But I will not charge fee from poor patients.

I hope my dispensary will be model for others doctors. They must realise that there is a greater need of doctors in village. Real India lives in villages. If health of villages is neglected, our country cannot make progress. Doctors must go to villages and nurse the suffering people crying for help.

VALUE OF DISCIPLINE

There is no life without discipline. It is discipline which fortifies the man with strong character, enlightens the mind with useful knowledge and instills in him the virtuous principles of life. It grants neatness and orderliness of life.

Discipline implies to prescribe a code of conduct. A student in the classroom has to maintain the discipline of listening quietly to his teacher. A son who disobeys his parents, a worker who disregards his superior, a soldier who goes against the rules of the army bring down upon himself the charges of indiscipline.

A man who lives in a social order has to subject himself to learn manners and follow certain rules. It is wrongly believed by the people that discipline imposes restrictions. To be truly free is to live under certain rules. Men who regard discipline as irksome fail to recognise that its absence leads to chaos. In every sphere of organised life, it is essential. Discipline is the most essential in games and sports. In all government offices and in the organisation of political parties, discipline is a great force; the success in commercial and industrial undertaking is activated by discipline. Discipline is a matter of human relationship. It means self control and it is self determination through self-direction.

At school or college we learn obedience to instruction and in office or at work regularity, punctuality and integrity of work. Hystorical mob tendency has jeopardised civic life. We must understand that on the one hand discipline is the basis of life and on the other a way to gain progress.

GOOD MANNERS

Manners are external expression of man's inner nature. The likes and dislikes, tastes feelings, temper and environment in which man lives are shown by his manners. Good manners are the mark of civility, decency and mutual accord. For man to live in the society, it becomes essential that he must have those qualities which find currency and are acceptable to other members of the society. In every society, certain practices come to be accepted as part of good manners. Although they are fine product of fine sensibility, education and upbringing may be manifest in numerous ways yet they provide the basis of peaceful and harmonious social life. Indeed, they are not forced upon anybody but the voluntary acceptance and their practice win for man admiration and sweet regard.

Good manners arise from a sense of courtesy. All genuine courtesy rises from sincerely of heart. The artificial rules of politeness and polish amount to snobbery and cannot be dispensed with truthfulness.

Without genuineness, life loses much of its freshness and much that makes it worthwhile. The courtesy is kindness and considerate feeling towards others. It seeks to contribute to the happiness of others. Politeness however, doesn't mean weekness of timidity. It is expected of a good natured man to be patient and tolerant to follies and foibles of others. To criticise, to condemn or even embarrass others does not behave a gentleman. Contradiction and refutations more often create bitterns and impair kindly relations. A man of good manners doesn't parade nor boast of his rank and achievements. He exhibits his character in performing rather than in boasting, in doing rather than in talking. Such man's conduct and behaviour become easy, free and spontaneous. He irradiates such an atmosphere of good temper and kindliness that he becomes an objective lesson to others in natural courtesy and good manners.

A cheerful person brings sunshine even in the gloomiest atmosphere. His conciliatory speech and good honoured bearing lends gaiety to all around him. Every day civilities of behaviour sweeten and general air. Manners are not born with us, they have to be learnt and acquired. A child must learn to be obedient to elders, to be fair entreating his equals and respectful to visitors to the house. Parents in this respect should not be over indulgent and should not pamper their children unreasonably.

Good manners are ornaments of a gentlemen. They are necessary for success and popularity in life.

GOD HELPS THOSE WHO HELPS THEMSELVES

Self help is a great virtue. It is the key to a successful life. It is a thing worth cultivating. Of course, we all require each others help. We are all dependent on one others help. But it does not mean that we should look helplessly to someone to do the work for us. Such a person is burden to his family and to the nation.

Dependence on others takes away our energy and initiative. We grow inactive lack confidence and eventually develop a sense of helplessness and disgust. A great measure of self-respect and honour is lost. Our own importance makes us miserable. We grow cynic and jealously poison our existence.

A self-reliant man is brave and determined and believes that good and bad conditions are result of the amount of labour one puts in his efforts. We trust no outside help expect no windfall but struggles with difficulties and hardships gathering and experience with every step.

He may succeed or fail but he is always an object of admiration and respect. The greatness of man depends trully upon his effort and not on success or failure.

He becomes the leader of men. Who look upto him and trust his capacity and wisdom. But it is not men alone who reward him three fourth, heaven also helps who helps him in his struggle. The heavenly helps comes in the form of pure joy which he feels in his heart for doing his duty.

Men of talent and other great personalities of the world have all been very industrious. They were the maker of their own destiny. Their example strengthens our belief in the motto "Self help is the best-help". God helps those who help themselves.

It is wrong on our part to magnify our obstacles and exaggerate our sufferings. To accuse fate, condemn chance and blame the stars is the acknowledgement of defeat. After all, "Man is the master of his fate".

THE HAPPIEST DAY OF MY LIFE

Students life is not a bed of roses. It means regular duties and hard work. A student has his own worries and moments of joy. He feels happy when he stands first in examination. He is worried when he fails. The winning of a prize is an occasion of great joy. The 23rd Oct. was the happiest day of my life. I shall always remember it. I received a number of prizes on that day.

On this day. Annual Prize Distribution function was held in our school. I was the most prominent figure on that day. I had stood first in the annual examination. I had won several first prizes in the sports. My principal declared me the best boy of the school. My teachers and classmates congratulated me. I felt a thrill of joy.

The Director of Education Mr. Verma, presided over the function. The Function was held in the spacious school hall.

It lasted for about three hours. The hall and the school compound were beautifully decorated. When the Director of education arrived, the N.C.C. boys presented him with the guard of honour. He was taken to the dias by our principal. The guardians of the students were also invited to the function. They sat on the seat on either side of the dias.

After sometime, a batch of small boys sang welcome song. The Principal then read out the annual report of the school. He said that the results of the school at public examination were very good. Then the prizes were distributed. The names of the prize winners were announced. They came on dias and received their prizes. As they received their prizes, there were clapping. Their faces showed happiness.

As I walked to the dias to receive the prizes, all the visitors and students clapped their hands. I got a medal and a set of books. A photographer took a photograph of me when I was receiving the prizes. It was the happiest day of my life.

HOBBIES

A hobby is a form of pastime which keeps us occupied during our leisure. If idle, we shall naturally, think of mischief. Hobbies enable us to spend our spare time delightfully and profitably. Constant hard work soon exhausts us.

A hobby provides us a welcome change and breaks the monotony of life. A man who has no hobby leads a dull and uninteresting life. He loses all zest and vigour for his work. One man's profession may be another man's hobby.

There are different types of hobbies. Stamp collecting is the commonest of all the hobbies. Some pursue photography. Others have riding, travelling or fishing as their hobby. Making penfriends is a good hobby. Some people have gardening as their hobby.

I have chosen stamps collecting as my hobby. It is a popular and international hobby. A number of books have been writing on it. There are stamps collecting societies in various countries. I was encouraged in this hobby by my uncle. I got my first collection of twelve stamps from him. At present, I have wonderful stamps album. It contains more than one thousand stamps of twenty different countries. I feel a sensation of romance and beauty when I look at it. It gives me a feast of different colours and designs.

The countries of the world bring out stamps of different colours, designs and shapes. Collection of these stamps gives me a great joy. My relations know my hobby. They send me rare postage stamps of different countries as gifts.

Sometimes, I have to spend money to purchase stamps of different countries. I have some pen friends in various countries. I exchange stamps with them.

Stamps collectng is of great value. Stamps have historical importance. They tell us about the cultures of the countries to which they belong. They also throw light on their social life. Sometimes stamps are issued to honour some great person or in memory of a great event. Some stamps give geographical information. They tell about the beauties of nature.

I am proud of my hobby.

HAPPINESS

"Happiness is but an occasional episode in the general drama of pain."

So says Hardy's herione Elizabeth Jane in the *"Mayor of Casterbridge."* But heppiness is neither an occasional episode nor is the general drama of life all painfull. Hapiness may elude us if we directly pursue it; it will come to us uninvited and stay with us if we do not give our mind to it.

Happiness is a condition of mind which keeps itself busy in work. The first codition of happiness is some kind of work in which we are absorbed. An active mind is an angle's workshop, just as an empty mind is the devil's workshop. We look before and after and pine for what is not, only when there is nothing to keep our mind engaged.

Our happiness depends on the kind of work what we pursue. Work that does not make us burn with desire is useless. So long as we are not in the work that we are doing, happiness will elude us. When our work engages all our being, when we are fully immersed in it, happines comes to us.

But the work that we take up should be such as may be worthy of our efforts. It should not be below our capacities. It is not good enough for a skilled farmer to spend all of his time in carrying dung, for a great scientist to give lessons in elementary physics or chemistry, or for a learned scholar to teach small children.

Happiness in itself is no object of pursuit. It is an incidental by-product of our activity. But we should not be engaged in selfish pursuits. That may make us misreable. It is only when we are devoted to a cause, when we work in co-operation with our fellow-beings, when we forget ourselves in the pursuit of a noble aim, an ideal in life, that we are happy.

"Another sound recipe for happiness in life ..... and do let us give a little thought tc the duty of being happy; there is no duty which we so persistently, under-rate is 'Nothing too much', which is one of the best known maxims of the Greek philosophers; to which I would add, 'Almost everything a little'?"

This is not making ourselves a Jack of all trades. It means, if properly understood and wisely practised, the fullest development of personality. It is to live a full life, which means to live a happy life. Let us obey all the demands of our nature.

This means that we should be the masters of our desires and not their slaves. This demands some discipline. This means not only to know where to stop but also to stop when we feel that we are not yet completely satisfied. A little unsatisfied desire before they are completely satisfied. "Don't smoke the last cigarett, don't drink the third glass of wine, and stop kissing the girl, while you and she are still ready for move."

Another important thing that can bring us happiness is to get interested in things. They will never deceive; they will never let you down. There may be very little sincerity in this world of men but in the world of things there is all sincerity. It was William Hazlitt who said, "There are only there pleasures in life pure and lasting-book, pictures, and the face of nature." Many other things like music, chess, eating and drinking may be added according to one's temperament and inclination. And so the last thing is to respect your own inclination and nature but do not allow it to run wild.

EQUALITY

The term 'Equality' is too often profaned. Its implication varies with every man who thinks of it. For example, with capitalists, it means an equal opportunity to exploit; naturally those who are in a position to exploit can use this opportunity. With democrates, it means 'one man, one vote'; thus an idiot and a lecturer are on equal footing. There are others who use this word as an excuse to treat all men as the clogs of a machine with no individualities of their own.

Equality if rightly understood consits in offering equal opportunities to all in the matters of education, civil rights, justice and physical, moral and intellectual progress. It becomes, however, impossible for any system of government to provide to the people equality in all these spheres unless their material well-being is not equally assured by a just economic system which ensures equitable distribution of the national wealth. Equality before law, for instance, has no meaning unless both the parties are in a position to employ the services of competent pleaders. Again, the rule that all the students are required to pay equal fees cannot be called just if some of them cannot pay them.

To be precise and brief, the problem of equality in all other spheres boils down to the question of economic equality ultimately. No streach of imagination nor any amount of practical manouverings can ever assure people that they are enjoying equality unless ecnomic equality is first guaranteed.

If we are assured of this fundamental truth, the next question that arises is the necessity of ensuring economic justice and enabling all people to give their best of the nation and to receive their just share in the national wealth. Under the present capitalistic system it is well high impossible that people may enjoy equal economic freedom or may have equal income. Since the means of production are owned and monopolised by the few rich men, the masses are generally employed in profitless job of making those rich men richer. It is hope against hope than these capitalists may undergo a change of attitude and a sense of equality and justice may prevail on them. They have acquired the power they hold by the force of 'Capital'. Unless some other equally potent force is used against them, they shall not part with their privileges, nor shall they ever willingly realise the injustice caused by them and their system to the humanity in general.

Thus the way to salvation lies through a system of nationalisation of industries and trade. The question of compensation and the place of labourers after nationalisation are unimportant questions comparatively and may be settled later. The existing lopsidedness in the society is definitely due to the unjust and in human practice of allowing certain individuals to have unrestrained freedom over the lives of the millions of people.

In the end, the moment we have an economic equality in the society, ever over kind of equality will naturally evolve and grow unimpeded, and our miserable world of today will be transformed into a world of righteousness, equality and liberty, where one will live and die for all and all will live and die for one.

NEIGHBOURS

Man is social animal. He desires a good company. Neighbours and the people with whom one lives becomes as the person himself is. If a person himself possesses the noble qualities of the fine feelings and sentiments, consistency, rectitude, self-sacrifice, honesty and truth, he is bound to create a happy atmosphere around him.

A good neighbour shares our joys and sorrows. He is not only kind and courteous but also hospitable and forbearing. A good neighbour feels that it is his duty to protect the honour and position of his neighbours. He visits us when we are sick. If we need money, he opens his purse to us. He is more than a friend or even a kind relative, for he is next door. In emergency, we can also seek his help and advice.

'Live and let live' should be guiding principle for communities and nations. As for individuals, it is a practical philosophy of life. To tolerate others to refrain from interfering with other and reconcile to the way of the others.

Mutual adjustment based on broad-minded attitude can create harmony and goodwill. It is this synthetic attitude of life which alone can make peaceful life possible.

TEENAGERS TODAY

Mahatma Gandhi's above words are highly meaningful and can inspire and present-day teenagers for good character, sound health, thinking and useful acts. For a sound mind, they should maintain sound body. Their acts should also be for social and national good.

The present-day position of our teenagers is far from satisfactory to be fast approching (arriving; coming). We often hear to a generation gap which is the cause of some of their problems. It is the need of understanding and adjustment which can bring about the solution of some of their problems. There is an urgent need for such solution for a realistic and needed social and national welfare.

We often near of examination boycott, cutting of classes and total strike by the students on schools and colleges. It is not only an educational headache but also a serious social problem. Its main cause is the faulty system of education which has been continuing in this country since the British rule in India. The present-day education is defective because it does not meet our social needs. The theoretical education which the students get today does not help them in earning their bread and butter (livelihood) tomorrow (in their future life). They are deprived of practical, occupational, or technical education which can be really helpful to them. The system of present day examinations is equally defective.

The problem of unemployment is another serious hindrance (obstacle) in the growth of our teenagers. The educated youths are roadmasters because they fail to get proper jobs. The more youths come out of colleges, the more serious this problem of unemployment becomes. The faulty system of education is mainly responsible for this problem. The rising population in the country has been making it more serious and complicated.

There is no need to be pessimist because there is always a 'silver-lining' for every problem. Some suggestions for the solution of their problems as well as for their necessary development are given in the following lines :

First of all, the present system of education should be changed and improved throughout the country. It should be made proper according to our social needs. The education of our teenagers and youths should help them in earning their bread and butter in their future life. They should be adequently given technical and occupational education. Their educations should be real and practical. It should also teach them the virtues of good character, good manners and social service. Only then they can prove useful citizens in their life.

Secondly, the present-day system of examination which is equally defective should also be fully changed and improved. There should be place for periodic evaluation, written work and ideal behaviour. The evils of cramming and copying must be rooted out.

Thirdly, the problem of unemployment should be solved in a real and practical way. The teenagers should be given useful and technical education which may help them in earning their living in future. For this, they should be given real education in science, commerce and literature.

Fourthly, there is an urgent need of understand between teenagers and their adults and elders. Some adjustments are neccessary and useful for both sides. Will the changing times, their needs and aspirations should be understood and fulfilled.

Lastly, India is chiefly a country of villages where there is a greater need of change and progress. An effective check on rural births must be put without delay. There family-planning should be spread in an effective way. Education should be given to all teenagers. Their co-operation should be taken in the good work of cottage industries by their family members. It shall help in the solution of unemployment.

Now it is the duty of elders to give importance to the needs, wishes and efforts of all teenagers. They, too, should get necessary guidance and inspiration from the experience and wisdom of their elders. Then we can hope for better society and stronger nation.

A FRIEND IN NEED IS A FRIEND INDEED

A good friend is a great blessing of God. They share our sorrows and double our joys. Neighbours and relatives feel jealous but friends always help. The miseries of life become tolerable with friends.

In life we depend on one another. Sometimes we want financial help and sometimes moral support. True friends stand by you through thick and thin. Friends have confidence in one another. They can make sacrifices.

False friends remain friendly during prosperous days only. They share your joys. But when you fall on evil days they desert. Some friends at the time of need, come out with excauses. We should not bother about such people.

Help from friends is not limited to human beings only. Even animals help their friends. We cannot live without this type of help.

There are so many problems in life. A person may fall ill or lose a job. He may fail in an examination. Enemies may become dominant. No one can face them single handed. We need some help. Only friends can give this help. If they ditch you at this time you are lost for ever.

You cannot expect a friend to be helpful if you are unhelpful. There should be mutual understanding. If friends doubt each other they can never give willing help. Such friends cannot excite friendly feelings.

A true friend is another self of man. He should respect the feelings of the other. He should place himself in the position of the other in order to understand his difficulties. Such a friend is a friend indeed.

FRIENDSHIP—BOON OR CURSE

Friendship in many respects is a boon. To a friend, we ventilate our feelings. If we do not express ourselves we develop tension in our mind. A friend doubles our joys and shares our sorrows.

There are certain secretes which a man cannot talk to any one except to friends. One can talk to his father with a sense of respect, one can talk to brothers and sisters with reservation but talking to a friend is free, frank and straight forward. That is why even the kings used to seek friends.

There can be lasting friendship only among unequals. Intellectually equal persons will never agree because their notions are formed before hand and their ideas have attained a sort of regidity. Equals will be the jealous of each other. Even friendship implies some sort of subordination by one of the other.

An officer should never be friends with a subordinate because they generally challange the authority of the man after knowing their secrets. Brutus was raised to his status by Caesar through friendship and Brutus was the person who killed Caesar.

Friendship cannot be based on mutual gain or loss. Such a friendship cannot last long because lost cannot be borne for a long time and gain cannot be tolerated by others.

Friendship is proper if the nature of the two persons is complementary and not contradictory nor contrary. One should complete the other and should not echo the qualities of the others.

Friendship can also be a curse. People have ruined their lives because they choose wrong friends. Such friends can do a lot of harm to the person either by misguiding him or by tempting him to bad habits.

HOPE

Hope is the main spring of human action. It cheers our way through the darkness of life. It acts as a balm to the injured hearts. It makes life interesting. A disappionted person will not do any work. It is the life blood of human soul.

If we entertain reasonable hope it serves as a tonic for man. But if we indulge in vain hopes we invite troubles. Foolish hopes are as bad as day dreams. He that lives on too much tope would die fasting.

If hope is helped by healthy imagination it will make the man the hero of the situation. But if hope are not supplemented with work it ruins. Thus hope is a double edged weapon. It may make a man wise or mad.

Hope if realised will lead to success and happiness. But if a man is ambitious his hopes do not die. If one's hope is realised he entertains many other. Only unhealthy minds do not hope. A scientist spends the whole of his life in research with the hope to discover or invent. A student works hard hoping to get good marks.

Hope is one of the greatest blessing of God. God has not revealed our future. We entertain hopes about the future. Had we known what would happen tomorrow we would never have hopes.

Sometimes our hopes cheat us. We hope to get something but we do not get. Even in such a situation one should entertain fresh hopes. Hopes are kept alive by many things. If you have faith in God you hope that God will help you. Similarly people having confidence keep their hopes alive. If your friends are healthy-minded they patronise your hopes. A little success at earlier stage also give life to hope.

HARD WORK

Work is worship. This beautiful universe is God's work. God himself is a worker. God wants man to work. Man has to work for earning his bread. He has to work for getting the comforts of life. He works to bring up his children. He also works to win fame and name. Work is born with man.

Hard work is not injurious to health. It is rather conductive to health. The labourers and farmers who do a lot of physical work enjoy good health. But the people who lie in their comfortable beds generally remain ill. Till the limbs of a man are not properly used man becomes an invalid. A machine may suffer wear and tear when used but not human body. In the 20th century science has given so many comforts that man has contracted a number of diseases.

Hard work is needed for body and mind. Mental work does not impair our mental faculties. Rather mental work makes mind keener and shaper. If you do not allow your brain to work you become dull.

One can do hard work if the person likes his work. Such a person gets a mental enjoyment. When you love your work you make a great progress. In our country the employment opportunities are so few that we do not get the work of our choice. In such a case one should added develop interest in the work.

Hard work determines our value in life. Idle people do not live properly. People do not like him. He is of no use to the society. Work is the condition of life. Hard workers have risen from the lowest position to the highest. Worth and work go hand in hand.

The reward of hard work in mental satisfaction. It gives peace to mind. Hard working people get sound sleep. They never develop bad habits because they remain busy. An idler is a burden on society. Man has brought heaven on earth through hard work.

IMPORTANCE OF LEISURE

Leisure is the free time one gets in the course of the day or after work for the day is over. In the hectic modern life of today, not everybody has time for leisure, and yet it is a very important part of life.

"All work and no play makes jack a dull boy" is very true in our modern civilization. Caught, as we are in a rat race, in this highly competitive, capitalist environment, it is all the more essential to get out of it for at least an hour or so and turn one's mind towards something else which is quite different from the daily grind of life.

Leisure provides rest and relaxation to our mind any body. To turn one's mind to something else that one enjoys doing, is a happy end to a day's hard work. One can then forget the tensions and pressures at one's place of work, and divert the mind in some creative and constructive manner.

There are different ways of occupying one's leisure hours. One can engage in a hobby which one enjoys such as reading, gardening stamp-collecting, photography, social work or anything else that one enjoys doing. Every such hobby enlightens the mind, since one is always learning something new. Reading broadens the outlook and often shows us a side of life that we have not been exposed to. Gardening, not only helps one to exert oneself physically, but teaches one appreciate the unique beauties of nature. Stamp-collecting arouses our interest in different countires and one learns a lot about them. Photography enables one to be creative and social work gives an immense satisfaction as one helps another to improve his life. Thus, every hobby provides a welcome relief from one's work. It is the one hour of the day when one can do what one has always wanted to do, but never finds the time to do in one's busy life. Infact, even cleaning up one's cupboard which one has not done for a long time, can be an interesting experience. One comes across objects might be linked to pleasant or unpleasant experiences and one can just sit and go down memory lane, which itself is a pleasurable experience. Finally, after one has cleaned up the cupboard, there is such an immense sense of satisfaction and achievement. Another usually long neglected occupation one can engage in is writing letters to people who have either written are waiting for a response, or to those who one should have written any way. This helps revive links and at the same time one has spent one's leisure time profitably.

Yet another way to relax is go out of the house—do window shopping or merely walk in a park and watch children play. Anything that is different from the daily routine and that one enjoys doing is a good way of spending one's leisure hours.

The importance of leisure can never be exaggerated. It helps one to "unwind" oneself and be healthy in mind and spirit. Infact, our forefather who were free from the tensions of modern life and had a leisurely way of life, were also free from the problems caused by stressful living such as highblood pressure, heart attack, brain haemorrage and so on. We, who cannot have a leisurely way of life should at least spare an hour of leisure. As W.H. Davies in his poem 'Leisure' so appropriately points out.

"A poor life this if, full of care,
We have no time to stand and stare."

LEISURE—ITS USE AND ABUSE

This is the age of machines. Machines do a lot of work for man. So the modern man gets a lot of free time. This leisure is used properly by some but other misuse it.

During leisure some pursue hobbies. This is perhaps the best use of leisure. Reading as a hobby adds to our knowledge. Playing games make us healthy mentally and physically.

Another good use of leisure is to do social service. It helps us to serve our society. It gives us a sort of satisfaction.

Some misuse leisure. They waste time by playing cards. Some gossip out their leisure. Sleeping during leisure time make us lazy and inactive. Now a days people use leisure by seeing films or listening to music. For a short period it may serve as a good pastime. But if it is a permanent feature it is dangerous.

Leisure is essential. Otherwise the work becomes dull. Henry Davies 'An English Poet' wants that we should have time to 'Stand and State'. But in the present day world we cannot waste time by just standing and staring.

It is suggested that if leisure is not used properly it is dangerous. Empty mind is devil's workshop. We should utilise our leisure properly and profitably.

THE MOST UNPLEASANT DAY IN MY LIFE

It was early last winter. I was returning from my school on my bicycle. As I reached bridge where five roads meet, I heard a uproar. I got down the bicycle and what I could see was a terrible scene. It has an accident, a cycle and motor lorry collision.

A young boy of about sixteen was run over by the motor lorry. It so happened that the boy was trying to cross the road from the left hand corner, suddenly a military truck arrived and collided with bicycle. The bicycle was completely smashed. The boy was lying dead in a pool of blood. The accident was very heart-breaking.

My blood boiled to see the condition of the boy. In a moment, a huge crowd gathered at the place of accident.

The driver of the military lorry was dragged down, the police who informed. On arrival of the police, the identity of the boy could be revealed. He was the son of the principal of a local college.

The police then asked the crowd to disperse as the traffic was blocked. I therefore, had to start for my home. I do not know what happened there afterward. But I still have suffocating memory of the accident. Whenever I pass through that crossing the same unpleasant accident comes to my memory.

MAN IS BORN FREE AND EVERY WHERE HE IS IN CHAINS

Nobody is more hopelessly enslaved than one who is under the false belief that he is free. By freedom we do not mean the right to vote, but also social, economic, domestic, mental and spiritual freedom. True liberty consists in the priviledge of enjoying our own right.

However it does not mean taking away the rights of others.

Our physical forces manifest itself in enslaving the weaker ones among us. Political domination leads to war and blood shed. Economics disparity leads to worst slavery of all where rich grow rich at the cost of poor. Poverty, hunger and starvation lead to slavery we suffer from inspite of our political freedom.

War are waged in the name of religion. Too much dependence of men on machines has turned him incapable of personal initiative. Spiritual bankrupty and growing materialism has made man slave to his work.

What light to the eye, what air is to the lungs, what love is to the human heart, liberty is to the soul of man.

AN UNWELCOME GUEST

A guest is worthy of our respect. This is what we are taught. But some guests are so troublesome that they are unwelcome. I had an unwelcome guest on 23 Oct. I was all alone in house. My parents had gone to attend a wedding. I stayed back as I was to take my Maths paper the next day. At about 4 o'clock there was a knock at the door. On opening the door, I found a middle aged man with his wife and three children. Before, I could recognise him and ask them in, they entered the room. He told me that he was my uncle.

And I was seeing this uncle of mine for the first time. He started a course of never ending conversation. I was worried all along about my examination. When my parents came home at 9 o'clock, I heaved a sigh of relief. I came to know that this gentle man and once met my father during a railway journey and got our address. May God save us from such unwelcome guests.

MY HOUSE

I live at Shastri Nagar in Meerut City. My father owes a house. It is in the heart of the city and every necessary thing is at a stone's throw.

There is a boundary wall around the main building. When we enter through the main gate we find big lawns on both sides of the passage. The flower beds run parallel on both sides to entrance. These lawns or gardens are very carefully maintained by my sister.

The main building is double storied. There are five rooms, kitchen, bathroom and latrine on the ground floor and three rooms on upper floor. As my father is principal, he has a visitors room. On right of the main entrance there is visitors room and on the left there is a drawing room. Bathroom are well-decorated with pictures, photos and scenery painted on the walls. There are three bed rooms and one store room. We are three brothers and one sister and so we have separate study rooms on the upper floor. There is a courtyard on ground floor.

My father, mother, elder brother and sister and myself complete the establishment. My elder brother and sister read in B.Sc. Final and B.A. Final respectively.

I like my home very much. It is very spacious and well-ventilated. It is comfortable in every season.

OUR NATIONAL PROBLEMS

POLLUTION

We are living in an age of grave ecological crisis-a-crisis which has been created by the imbalance between the population, resources and environment. A biological community is a balanced community. Its successful survival depends upon the inter-action and inter-relationship between the physical environment and the living beings themselves.

In order to increase food production man has used powerful synthetic pesticides and inorganic fertilizers. Such modern farming practices have brought in the Green

Revolution but have caused serious environment problems. The non-biogradable chlorinated hydrocarbons like D.D.T. used as pesticides are found in every living plant and animal around the world.

The crises of population verses food and resources alone would be a massive challenge for humanity to face over next twenty to thirty years. Rapid industrialization and modern technology have led to a serious deterioration in environment.

As a factor in human health and well-being, environment pollution is a serious cause for alarm, specially in developed countries where the most of it is produced.

Air pollution in highly industrialised cities had led to an increase in respiratory diseases. It damages trees and crops as well as human tissues.

Water pollution also poses a serious threat. The common pollutants in the waste rare insecticides, industrial waters, sewage, fertilizers and other kinds of wastes. Polluted waters can cause and spend large number of water borne diseases.

Modern life has become very noisy. The noise of traffic in big cities and aeroplanes and noisy machines all take their toll in affecting the human hearing apparatus and reducing the efficiency. People exposed to radio active substances are likely to develop cancer.

Mans impact on environment has reached a state when "pollution" in usual sense is only a part of the problem. His activities now present a grave danger to the entire planet Earth which nourished and supports us all.

CORRUPTION

It is said that Corruption is the handmaid of democracy. Leaders who spend lakhs on elections want to earn crore when elected. This sets in the vicious circle of corruption. Society degenerates and political stability is endangered.

Prof. Leslie Palmier has conducted a very comprehensive study of the malady of corruption. He has advocated the drastic change in the social structure. In the older fendal order status and function of a person was determined by birth. But to day, both function and status have come to be associated with the wealth. The palatial houses and luxury cars have become the status symbals. Moral values have lost their credibility. Material gains have become the ultimate goals. This has shattered the moral edifice of our society.

Those who give money to the candidate for contesting elections expect to be rewarded. The process has given birth to crafty and greedy politicians bereft of political philosophy and moral aim. The remedy for politico-electoral corruption is to have indirect election and proportional voting. Another suggestion is the clearer demarcation of functions of the executive and the legistature. There is also a need for greater autonomy for bureaucracy. The Judiciary should be paid higher salaries.

Roots of Corruption lie in providing opportunities to be corrupt. Public servants should never be allowed to control commercial activities. Officers recognise that it is hard for their subordinates to live on the small salaries. So they condone corruption.

THE PROBLEMS OF FLOOD

Floods in India are a common experience. Sometimes we get too much rain, and sometimes not at all. Sometimes our rivers overflow their banks. Sometimes they get dry. Nature seems to play tricks on human beings.

Floods bring in their wake misery and destruction. Standing crops are destroyed, houses swept away, men and animals drowned. The whole area is covered by one white sheet of water and people have to run to safer places. Sometimes flood waters catch the people unawares. In such circumstances they have to take shelter on tree tops or roofs of their houses. It is common to see snakes also floating in flood waters. Some snakes also curl sound trees and find shelter there along with human beings.

This is not the end of the miseries of flood-stricken people. For days together people cannot be evacuated. They cannot be supplied with food. The Government has to do a lot of work to evacuate them. Even then many people and thousands of live stock perish. Flood waters sometimes in this fury wipe out the entire villages leaving behind no trace of their existence.

The Government is trying its best to control floods. Many dams are being built and many other ways adopted to divert the surplus waters to other useful purposes. Yet floods occur every year and bring destruction to human life, cattle and trees.

Floods in India and everywhere else are a natural calamity. Their devastating effect can, however, be mitigated by people's co-operation. Only if the villagers agree to leave for good their villages which are situated in flood belts, much of the loss can be avoided.

Like so many other things floods have another important side also. These destroy everything in their wake but increase the fertility of the soil. As Mr. Nehru once remarked floods are a blessing in disguise. Vast tracts of fields which otherwise remain dry get drenched in flood waters and become capable of producing bumper crops. Even then it is poor consolation. Floods undoubtedly do more harm than good.

DRUG-ADDICTION

Drug have caught the fancy of our youngmen and women. This is a matter of serious attention and grave concern. This implies physical dependence upon a drug. An addict requires more and more quantity of the drug to transport him to the world of fantasy.

The metropolitian cities of India are in the vicious grip of drug menace. It is telling upon the physical and mental health of our young men and women.

Addicts mainly use the narcotics, hullucinagens, stimulants and sedatiues, marijuana and amphatamines are all habit forming drugs. The drug addict loses all sense of time, place and person. Hallucinations and delusions may also follow. Abberations in perception are quite marked.

Drugs intake dilates pupils of the eyes, flushes the fall, raises the body temperature and accelerates the heart-beat.

Sometimes blood pressure shoots up followed by convulsions and fits. Drugs are supposed to increase alertness and vigour but their effect is short timed. Medically, drugs are used to reduce depression. Taken with out medical supervision, people tend to take over doses and this may lead to addiction. Barbituarates if taken with narcotics can prove fatal.

Drug addiction is malody of gigantic propertion. Its tentacls eat into vitals of our society. It can play havoc with life of a person. It can ruin its family. The personality of the addict is dwarfed. The people and the Government should make a concerted effort to root out this evil by checking the diabolic trafficking in drugs.

A THEFT

It was the month of March. All the members of our family had gone to Delhi to attend the Marriage ceremony of my cousin. I did not go with them because I had to take my English examination the next day. I was all alone in my house and studied late at night.

I went to bed at 12 in the night. I had hardly slept when I heard a sound in the adjacent room. I silently rose and crept out of my room. I saw some light in the room of my mother. When I looked into the room I saw a thief who was opening the jewellery box of my mother. I was much afraid but I didn't lose courage. I hid myself behind the wall near the door of the room.

The thief broke open the jewellery box, took out ornaments and put them into his pocket. He then turned to the other box. Now his back was facing the door. I did not miss the chance and tip told to the door. I shut it and bolted it from out.

Then I began the shout at the top of my voice, "thief, thief, help mc." Hearing the cry, the neighbours rushed into my house. I told them what had happened. One of them ran to call the police. Immediately one inspector of police with two constables came into my house and opened the door. They found the thief and took him away to police station. They returned me the ornaments obtained from the thief.

When my father and mother came back they praised me very much and embraced me.

GENERAL ESSAYS

THE POSTMAN

The postman is a Government servant. He is a very useful and popular person. Everybody knows him well. He is always welcomed.

He wears khaki uniform. He has a turban on his head. He has a leather bag. He keeps letters, parcels and money-orders in it. He has another bag in which he keeps bigger packets and parcels.

He can read and write English, Hindi and Urdu well. He works very hard. It may be hot or cold or rain but he has to do his job. He goes to the post office early in the morning. There he sorts the letters and goes from door to door to deliver them. Hc brings us letter, parcels and money-orders.

He brings us both good and bad news. He is very gentle and honest. He is regular, punctual and trusted person. He speaks gently. He is very careful in doing his duty. He is active and polite. But on festival days, we offer him money and he accepts it gladly. He is a low paid servant. He gets a few holidays.

His life is very hard. So his condition is very miserable. He has to cycle long distances in all kinds of weather. He takes much trouble to do his work. Therefore, the government should increase his pay so that he may support his family well. We have every sympathy for him.

NEWSPAPERS

A free press is a sign of cultured and democratic freedom. Newspapers hold the density of the nation in their hands. Today newspapers have become almost as necessary as food and clothing. It does a great service by bringing us news from every corner of the world. A newspaper caters to the needs of the various sections of the society.

It furnishes information and enlarges our mental horizon. It is great education of the public mind. The present to us a true picture of the tendencies in the market. Newspapers also keep us informed about east developments in every field. They develop in us a flair for reading and writing.

But newspapers have their dark side too. Some are becoming willing tools in the hands of vested interests. They do not place true facts before the public. So we should practice independent judgment while reading a newspaper. They often corrupt the tastes of their readers. Newspapers are often partial to particular political parties or personalities.

Newspapers should avoid these. They should use their privilege with great care and caution. They should act as guardian of public interest. They should realise their social and political responsibilities.

CINEMA

Modes of entertainment have undergone a revolutionary change. Today the most popular form of recreation is cinema. Its phenomenal popularity and development is due to its mass appeal.

A motion picture based on a classical novel will induce thousands of people to re-read the book. The man of today is better informed than his ancestors due to cinema.

The political awareness fight for the rights and general awakening of masses is largely contributed by cinema.

Cinema has also thrown down the barriers of time and space. It has made man truly cosmopolitan in outlook. A grand sight in cold Norway is reproduced vividly to people in hot Africa. A political or social revolution in one part of the country is shown the world over.

Cinema has opened up a lucrative profession. Besides encouraging youngmen and women to enter the field of acting in films, it has provided employment to thousands of women and men as technicians, designers, photographers, actors, actresses, dress-makers and various allied agencies.

Film artistry is unfortunately, compelled to compromise with people's popular taste and appeal to their lower instincts. Too many films dealing with sex problems and with the ways of the criminals are now shown. These are apt to affect public morality.

The films make the young prematurely sex conscious, andalism and increasing acts of rowdyism in the student community are attributed to their indiscriminately frequenting the cinema halls.

They grow divorced from harsh and dismal realities of life and start living in a fairy land picturised on the screen.

Cinema has tremendous possibilities in our country. With our abundant natural wealth and high literature, our cinema has a great future.

A MAGIC SHOW

One day a magician showed us many tricks. A small boy was with him. The magician put a basket on the floor. The boy sat under it. He cut the basket with the sword. After a little while the boy came out alive. This was his first trick.

Then he took a jug full of water. He poured the water into a bucket. Then he put the empty jug on the table. He lifted the jug and it was full of water. Everybody wondered at it. He poured the water into the bucket again. When the bucket was full, he put the lid on the bucket. He lifted the lid and the bucket was full of burning flames.

We all liked this trick. His last trick, was very interesting. He burnt five-rupee note. Then he broke an egg.

A piece of bread came out of it. He cut the piece and found in it the five rupee note. Every body clapped and laughed.

MUSIC

"The light of thy music illumines the world. The life breath of thy music runs from sky to sky. The holy stream of thy music breaks through all stony obstacles and rushes on."

—Rabindranath Tagore

According to Spencer, music is an aid to the achievement of higher happiness. It takes rank as the highest of the fine arts, as the one which more than any other, ministers to human welfare.

Music is one of the fine arts; as dance is an artistic expression of movement and painting of colours, so music is of sounds. What a pretty sight is to the eyes, aroma is to the nose, delicious dish is to the palate and soft touch is to the skin, so music is to the ears.

According to Plato, one of the eminent Greek philosophers, music is an important aspect of education. In his scheme of education, he has laid emphasis on three disciplines—Gymnastics for the training and development of the body, Mathematics for the training and development of brain and Music for the realization of the soul.

"Music is a moral law. It gives soul to the universe, wings to the mind, flight to imagination, a charm to sadness, gaiety and life to everything." ***—Plato***

Love for music is a characteristic, not only of man but of nearly all living creatures. The moment musical notes softly enter our ears, they rouse the dormant love for it. Mythology as well as folk tales bear evidence to the fact that even animals respond with joy to the melodious vibrations of the harp. The cows used to respond to the call of Lord Krishna's flute and flock round him when it was time to return home.

Music has unlimited powers, is a well established fact. It has a soothing and healing power. Just as the application of balm relieves our brain of its ache and tension, so music can relax the tense muscles of our body. The melodious notes of music have the capacity to cure the mental or physical fatique of a weary person.

Music has miraculous powers for treating certain mental ailments such as abnormal excitement or depression. It is helpful for the treatment of patients suffering from insomnia. It has excellent exhilirating power. It can be compared to mother's love. Just as a child forgets everything and feels joy in mother's lap, in the same way we forget all worries and anxieties in musical environment.

Music has magical power, is testified by the fact that Orpheus, a well-known Greek musician could make stones dance to his music. The stories of Tansen and Baiju Bawra are not unknown to us. They could light lamps, melt stones, blossom flowers in autumn, cause rain just by the accurate use of the 'swaras'. These are not tales but facts which can be well supported by such thoughts : *"Music hath charms to soothe a savage breast, to soften rocks, or bend a knotted oak."* Congreve.

There is no doubting the various powers of music, but the aspect of music which is of the greatest value to the human being is its emotional aspect. No achievement can be so great as the emotional and spiritual uplifting that we get from music.

Music washes away from the soul, the dust of everyday life and inspires one to live a lofty life. When the 'swara' enters one's heart there is transquilty and harmony which can only be tasted when one has such an experience. The notes of music take the listener to the region of the unknown where there is only emotional ecastacy and transport him to a world of melody and sympathy.

CRICKET : THE BIGGEST SPORT OF OUR COUNTRY

A lot of things in our life which gives us entertainment and refreshment and in these things sports have their own importance. We have a lot of sports in the world like Hockey, Cricket, Chess, Badminton, Lawn Tennis, Motor Cycle race, Car race, Horse riding, Cycling, Swimming, Football, etc. In all these sports every sport have their own craze and importance. The craze of every sport is streched in different-different parts of world. In Indian sub confinent where India, Pakistan, Srilanka, Nepal, Bangladesh, etc. is situated. Cricket is the biggest sport. In all these countries cricket is like a religion. In those countries when any cricket match play then a situation like curfew is streched everywhere nobody wants to leave the match. Every person whether a child, youngman, ladies, oldman wants to see the match. We can easily see the T.V. sets on shops, offices and all business institutions where people gathers to see the match. Those people who unable to see the match on T.V. sets they used radios and transisters to hear the match commentary and enjoy the match. The ladies also enjoys the cricket match in houses. The people of cities can enjoy match on T.V. but in interior villages where T.V. not available people uses radios, but does not want to miss the match. In India Cricket is like a religion, Cricket is the one of main thing which make our country united. This craze and enthusiasm for Cricket encourage the players of Cricket and this enthusiasm also promote the companies to sponser the Cricket team and players.

THE VALUE OF GAMES AND SPORTS

Today we are living in the age of science which has given us a large number of discoveries and inventions. They have become part the parcel of our life. We are overbusy with the work of earning and spending. Such hurry and worry has created much mental tension. The present-day students are weak in body and mind. The load of their study is reponsible for it.

There is a great study value of games and sports for all students and other young person. Only study all the time is not enough because "All work and no play makes jack a dull boy." It is a correct saying that games and sports are very necessary for the development of physical and mental powers. Those students who take an equal and active part in games and sports also show brilliant results in their examinations. The yougths have extra energy which should be used in games and sports. In this way, they will be more disciplined and useful.

The chief advantage of games and sports is that they afford (give) much pleasure and recreation. In the present day world of much hurry and worry all students and other young boys and girls should get adequate (enough) pleasure and recreation. Thus they can pay real and greater attention to their study and other serious work. There is already much sorrow and suffering in our life which should be made carefree and happy. For this we should get pleasure and recreation by taking an active part in games and sports. In short, games and sports are an important source of pleasure, recreation and happy life.

Physical and mental development is another important advantages of games and sports. It is a very popular saying that "a sound mind lives in a sound body." Those students who regularly take part in games and sports make the useful development of their body and mind. Then they can study well and achieve (get) true success in their future life.

Our students and other boys and girls can learn much discipline by taking part in games and sports regularly. It is perfectly true that a playground is the best place to teach discipline to our youths. In this way, they can prove useful social units and good citizens in their adult life. There is the want of discipline everywhere and it can be successfully achieved by games and sports which have been gaining ground by leaps and bounds (very rapidly) in this country.

Group life is another important advantage which our students and young persons learn from game and sports. Group life is much developed when boys and girls participate (take part) in games and sports. They also learn and virtues of group life, co-operation and working unitedly. They play and work with love and affection. It creates in their mind a useful sense of social and national service. For such useful group life games and sports have significant value.

Young boys and girls have an extra amount of youthful energy which is sublimated (used well) through games and sports. In this way, our youths become more disciplined and useful citizens in their future life. If this energy is not utilized in this way, our youngmen may turn into thieves, pick-pockets and other types of criminals. With this reason, there is a great need of games and sports for our students and other young boys and girls. It shall bring about social and national betterment.

It is a happy news that games and sports have been rapidly developing in our country. It is the need of the hour and our government should give necessary encouragement and financial aid. They shall help in human and national good in the end.

MOUNTAINERRING

Mountains have been fascinating man. Mountains climbing is a sport full of romance and adventure. It does not suit all men. Only those who have love for danger and adventure can derive pleasure from it. **Blake** has rightly said "Great things are done when men and mountains meet."

The sudden unexpected change in the weather pose a serious problem. The strong wind and snow blast. Walking on snow is really very tough. In case snow is hard the climbers have to cut steps which is quite exhausting sometimes snow is soft and they sink deep into it.

Mountain-climbing is a technique. It requires proper training, skill and knowledge. They must know to use maps compasses oxygen-apparatus and other equipments. Apart from physical strength moral and spiritual values along with team work are very essential.

They must travel through dense woods as they approach a mountain and cross-step stoops and rock study about the tree line on mountain. In dangerous areas, climbers rope themselves together in groups.

There are mountaineering clubs where training is imparted to the members. A mountaineering institute at Darjeeling has been established under the expert supervision of Tenzing to develop interest of mountain climbing among Indians. Indian montaineers have succeeded in conquering the Everest under the leadership of Lt. Col. M.S. Kholi.

Mountain climbing is a thrilling adventure which brings about the heroic quality of man's body and mind.

MODERN MEANS OF RECREATION

The present age is the period of science which has given us numerous discoveries and inventions which have become the part and parcel of our life. We are so used to them that we cannot live without them now. The present age shows the ear (period) of change and progress in a large measure.

In the past too, there were games, sports, musical programmes and theatical shows for the recreation of common people. Kings and Emperors were pleased and entertained by their court singers, jesters and brave wrestlers.

In the present-day world the made of recreation has fully changed. It is because of the invention of the means of recreation like cinema, radio and television. They are briefly described in the following lines for common information and knowledge.

Cinema is the most popular and cheapest means of recreation to all men, women and children in the present age. After a day's hard work, an entertaining film at a popular cinema house removes all mental strain and worries. A man, or a woman feels tension free, pleased and entertained after enjoying a film in the evening. The popularity of cinema can be easily seen by the long queues the booking-window and fully full cinema halls. Cinema is popular in big cities, small towns and even in big fairs, etc.

Radio is the second popular means of recreation. It is equally popular both in urban and rural areas. Even a farmer, or a factor worker owns (has) it for his recreation. It gives us music, news, short dramas, educational programmes and commentary of games and sports. Really a radio is a very popular means of pleasure to us.

Television is the most modern means of recreation to a large number of men, women and children. The television sets are still very costly, so they are out of the reach of common and poor village people. India is mainly a country of villages were a major part of our population lives. With this reason, it should be the best efforts of big industrial producers as well as of our government to supply television sets at a lower and reasonable price to the village people. It is the need of the hour in the present age of science and progress. A television shows also the face of a singer, player, news- reader, etc. 'Chitrahaar', popular-serials and weekly films give much pleasure and recreation to men, women and children. There are more and more programmes on games, sports and education. Cable and disc televisions are the latest achievements.

Games and sports are also an important and popular means of recreation in the present age. They are becoming more and more popular among boys and girls of the country. The game of cricket has become very popular in the country in recently years. During test matches of cricket, all men, women and children take much interest, pleasure and recreation in their radio or T.V. commentary. The young boys even neglect their food and both in the days of such commentary. The names of Sunil Gavaskar, Azhar-ud-din and Kapil Dev are very dear and well-known to them. As means of recreation, games and sports are becoming more and more popular.

It is sad and bad that some students neglect their study because they are over-interested in cricket, games or sports. There is the need of balance between the two. Both serious work or study and recreation are needed by us for a better and fuller development of our personality.

❑❑❑

LETTER WRITING

LETTER-WRITING

Letter-writing is an art like painting or sculpture. It is perhaps the oldest means of communication. The letter is the easiest and simplest form of communication between two persons or bodies of persons. Letter-writing plays an important role in the lives of men. Its incrcasing importance as a branch of modern education is being recognised in our schools and colleges.

Letters may either by private or public while private letters deal with homely or familiar correspondence, public letters are invariably formal communications. The two important things in the production of a good letter are matter and manner. What we write about and how we write it are the fundamental features of letter-writing. The best way of letter-writing consists in expressing simply and directly appropriate ideas in an essay, simple and elegant style. Good mood and tranquil mind are necessary for getting right ideas and good thoughts. Hence for writing important letters good temper is a must.

Types of Letters. Letters may be divided into three main categories :

(1) Private Letters,

(2) Official Letters and

(3) Business Letters

(1) Private Letters. The letters which we write to our relatives or friends are private letters. These letters are about personal matters.

(2) Official Letters. Letters that we write to offices or receive from them, are called official letters. These letters deal with official matters.

(3) Business Letters. Letters that we write to firms or traders or receive from them are called business latters.

The parts of a letter :

(a) **The address of the writer.** It is written at the top towards the right side, as

121, Pan Bazar,
Guwahati.

(b) **The date of writing.** The date of writing should be given in full. It is written below the address, as,

15, Curzon Road,
New Delhi.

6th January, 2004

(c) **Salutation.** It is written towards the left of the page. A comma is always placed at its end. The first and the last word begin with capital letters as,

(1) **Private letters.** My dear Father, My dear Sister, My dear Friend. My dear Richa, My dear Divya.

(2) **Official letters.** Sir/Madam.

(3) **Business letters.** Dear Sir, Dear Sirs, Gentlemen, Madam.

(d) **Body of the letter.** This is the most important part of the letter. It contains the message. The writer should use simple and easy words.

(e) **Subscription.** It comes at the end of the letter. Forms of Subscription in different kinds of letters are :

(1) Private letters.

(a) To relation. as,

Your affectionate mother, Your loving Son, Your affectionately.

(b) To friends. as,

Your Sincere friend, Yours sincerely, Your truly.

(c) To strangers. as,

(2) Official letters.

Your faithfully

(f) Address.

The address of the person to whom the letter is sent, is written on the envelope as,

Mr. B. R. Sharma
73, Lachit Nagar,
Guwahati.

MODEL LETTERS

➤ **1. Write a letter to your father. Tell him about your School.**

Springdales Public School,
Happy Valley,
Shillong.

12th January, 2004

My Dear Father,

I was very happy to read your letter. I promise to act upon your advice. All my classmates are nice girls. Some are noisy but all of them are sincere. So far, I do not know much about them. My class master is very kind to me. Our School has good library. I have taken out from the library some new books about sea-stories.

I will write home every week. With love to mother.

Your loving daughter,
Divya

➤ 2. To a Bookseller ordering Book.

D. A. V. School,
Rohtak.

22nd January, 2004

To,

M/s. Modern Book Depot,
Educational Publishers,
Karol Bagh, New Delhi-110 005

Dear Sirs,

I shall feel obliged if you send me a copy of the following books per V. P. P. at your earliest convenience.

(1) The Advanced Learners Dictionary of Current English.

(2) New English Essays and Letters.

(3) English Course for Secondary Schools, Parts I and II.

Yours truly,
Mahender Bhargava

➤ 3. Write a courteous letter to your neighbour whose radio disturbs you.

D-6, Lajpat Nagar,
New Delhi.

26th January, 2004

My dear Mr. Barman,

I am, indeed, very sorry to inform you that I am being constantly disturbed in my studies by your radio which is kept on at loud pitch at all hours.

You know that I am taking the Senior Certificate Examination this year and therefore need concentration in my work.

May I request you therefore to keep your radio at a lower pitch. I hope you won't mind this little inconvenience.

Thanking you.

Yours sincerely,
Nidhi

LETTERS

➤ **1. Write a letter to your father requesting him to allow you to accompany a party of students going on an educational tour.**

Karol Bagh,
New Delhi.

14th January, 2004

My dear Father,

Our school is organising an educational tour to some of the historical places of Rajasthan. The party will visit Jaipur, the pink city, Udaipur and its fine lake and Chittore, where the famous Rana Pratap fought with the Mughals. Our Principal and a senior teacher of History will accompany the party.

The party will proceed on tour on the 25th instant and return on the 31st. The total expenses for the tour have been estimated at Rs. 300/- per head. The school will contribute half of this amount. This tour will be of great educational value.

So I shall request you to allow me to join the party.

With regards.

Your loving son,
Rajesh

➤ 2. Write a letter to your father from the hostel about your progress in studies.

56, Vikash Vihar,
New Delhi.

29th January, 2004

My dear Papa,

You will be glad to learn that I am doing quite well in my studies. When I left home, I was weak in 'English and Hindi'. But after arriving here I told my teachers about my weakness in these subjects. They were so good that they called me in their spare time and removed all my difficulties. From the letter I am writing to you it should be clear that my English is no longer what it is used to be.

I am now trying hard to make up my deficiency in Maths. I have approached my subject teacher for his advice and he had recommended some books.

You and Mummy can rest assured that this year my result will not let you down.

Please do keep me in touch with everything at home. Kindly convey my regards to dear mother and my love to Shashi.

With regards.

Yours affectionately,
Priya

➤ 3. Your father is in Government service and has been transferred outside Delhi recently. Write a letter to him describing how you are helping the household.

114, Shastri Nagar,
New Dehli.

16th January, 2004

My dear Father,

I received your letter yesterday. We are happy to know that you have liked your new place of posting.

You needn't worry about us. All of us are quite well. I get up early in the morning and study for 2 hours. In the evening, I help mother in bringing the daily necessities.

Rita has stood first in the college by securing 73% marks. She would be joining B.Ed. I am busy preparing for the N.D.A. and C.P.M.T.

Grand mother is better now. Of course she is taking her medicine regularily. Dear mother is perhaps feeling very lonely. Uncle Gulshan often comes to look after us.

Didi Urmil has come back from the States. Hope she will be writing to you. Please don't worry about us at all. Mother wants you to be cautious in your evening meals and drinks.

With love from grandma and regards from us.

Yours affectionately,
Suhel

➤ 4. A letter to son giving a good advice by father.

45, Shardha Puri,
Meerut.

My dear Son,

I am really happy to learn that you have been making satisfactory progress in your studies, particularly in Mathematics and Science. You should not neglect languages at all. As you are weak in English you will work hard giving special care to grammar and spellings to make up your deficiencies in that subject. Your examination is fast approaching hence you give more attention to your studies.

Do not think that if you work hard burning midnight oil just a few days before the examination you will get success. On the other hand, steady and regular work day after day and week after week from the beginning of the year will bring you assured success.

Please avoid idle or bad company. Associate with good and diligent boys. Also maintain good health by taking nutrition and hygenic food. I am sending you 300/- Rs. to cover all your expenses. Write to me often about your health and progress you have made in your studies.

Your loving father,
Ramesh Kumar

➤ 5. Write a letter to your elder brother. Request him to take you to Simla.

28, Defence Colony,
New Delhi.

20th January, 2004

My dear Brother,

Our school will break up from Monday, for one month. It is very hot in Delhi. I think it is cool at Simla. Life is very dull here. It must be very pleasant at Simla. I have never been to Simla. Please take me to Simla for a change. The climate of Simla is good for health. We can go for long walks daily.

I am sure we will come back fresh and fine.

I hope you won't disappoint me.

Yours affectionately,
Nidhi

➤ 6. Write a letter of advice to your younger brother who is about to appear in the examination.

23, Kamla Nagar,
New Delhi.

23rd January, 2004

My dear Vinay,

I have just received your letter. You have written that your annual examination is at hand and that you are not satisfied with your preparation.

But I feel that you are a bit nervous. I am sure you will fare well because you have been regular in your studies. Do not lose heart and try to get rid of this phobia.

Revise what you have already learnt. Be confident. Nothing can be achieved without courage. Get up early in the morning to study. Do not panic. Take time to think over what you have studied. This will help you to remember well.

Pray to God daily. You shall feel strengthened. Write to me after your examination is over.

With best wishes.

Yours elder brother,
Harish Gupta

➤ **7. Write a letter to your brother/sister that you do not feel lonely, though you are away from home, for the first time. Describe some new friends and sorroundings you are in.**

Sherwood College,
Nainital.

28th January, 2004

My dear Raju,

I feel quite happy here. Although I am away from home for the first time, yet the atmosphere and the routine of this institute does not let me feel home-sick.

I am sorry to note that you are needlessly worrying about me. Undoubtedly I felt home-sick for some days but now I have adapted myself to the new life.

My classes are held from 8.15 to 2.30, we have lunch at 1 p.m. then there are other activities. The teachers keep us busy all day long.

I take part in the morning physical drill, evening games and other activities of the school. The Superintendent of the hostel is very painstaking and loving. We live here like the members of a family.

I have made some good friends here. One is a magician with numbers. He always gets 100% marks in Maths. His name is Fernandes. The other one is a poet. He writes very good Hindi poetry and recites it well. Even our teachers are impressed by him. He is Gyanprakash from Meerut. The third is Firoz who is the best football player in our school. He comes from Nagaland. The fourth is Mohindra Singh who is the best athlete in the whole school.

Please convey my regards to Mummy and Daddy and assure them I am quite happy here.

With best wishes.

Yours affectionately,
Ranjan Majumdar

➤ **8. Write a letter reprimanding in your younger brother who has fail in almost all the subject.**

12/2, Shastri Nagar,
Meerut.

31th January, 2004

My Dear Viney,

I am greatly shocked to go through your Progress Report Card received the other day. You have failed almost in all the subjects. This is a matter of utmost shame and regret.

I have never expected such a bad performance from you. What has gone wrong. You are so intelligent and working. Perhaps it is lack of responsibility on your part.

From this report one can infer that you are not paying due attention to your studies.

Last Sunday, your class teacher Mr. Gupta met me in the Company Garden. He tole me that you have become a drug-addict. You often bunk classes and loiter around. This does not behave you. You should not waste your precious time.

You are a good boy. I hope you will mend your ways and be serious about your studies. I advice you to give me no chance of complaint.

With love.

Yours affectionately,
Vishal Ahuja

➤ 9. Write a letter to younger brother advising him how he should improve his health.

525/3, Indira Colony,
Ita Nagar.

3rd January, 2004

My dear Prasay,

I am very sad to learn from dear mother that you have not been keeping good health this year. Often you have fallen sick with fever or cold. Why is it so? Have you tried to analyse the reason?

I feel the reason is over work. I appreciate that you are working very hard. But Board Examination doesn't mean that you neglect your health. Without good health, substained effort can not be made in any direction.

So do spare some time for exercise. A morning walk shall certainly do you good. Be careful about your diet. Take plenty of citrus fruit. These built up resistence and stamina. Avoid taking too much of coffee or tea.

I hope if you follow a routine of work with leisure, you shall have the pleasure of good health.

Yours affectionately,
Firoz Khan

➤ 10. A model letter written by R. Krishna to his brother informing about his school.

Subhash Puri,
Meerut.

1st January, 2004

My dear Brother,

You will be glad to hear that I am now attending Dewan Public School which is considered the Premier Secondary School in this city.

My school is a spacious building with many well-verntilated class rooms. Our play-ground is not far from our school. We play foot-ball and cricket in the evening hours.

Our principal is an experienced M.A., B.Ed., and takes very interest in every thing connected with his institution.

Expecting an early reply.

Your affectionate brother,
Vikas Goswami

➤ 11. Write a letter to your younger brother advising him to take part in games rather than be a book worm.

Sector-I Shastri Nagar,
Meerut.

20th January, 2004

My dear Mukesh,

I am very much pleased to learn about your brilliant success. At the same time, I am pained to learn about your ailment. It means that you have worked at the cost of your health. It is really a bad bargain.

I really appreciate your ambition to get position in the Board Examination. But, you should devote proper time to games also. It is not good to become a book-worm. You should remember that a healthy mind can live only in a healthy body. Games cultivate discipline and team spirit also.

Work is not doubt worship but over-work is injurious to both brain and body. Brain needs relaxation also. Do spare sometime for games also.

Let studies and sports go side by side.

Your affectionately,
Rakesh Kumar

➤ **12. Write a letter to your uncle thanking him for the birthday Gift.**

21, Kalkuchi
..... City
23rd January, 2004

My dear Uncle,

Thank you for the wonderful present you have sent me this time on my birth day. All my friends have liked it very much.

To tell you the truth, I needed a wrist watch very badly I was often late for School. I hope this new watch will regulate my life. It will help me to be punctual. Its black dial with golden floor and hand looks very attractive.

It is token of your love and affection for me. I shall keep it with utmost care. Sister Urmil had given me a Parker 51 and Father a Hero Puck. With all these things, I am feeling on top of the world.

But I do realise that I have now to work extra hours to meet your expectations.

I once again thank you for the nice present.

With regards.

Your loving nephew,
Atul

13. Preeti is Balbir's friend. She has written a letter to Balbir. Her letter is given below :

21, The Mall,
Shimla.

14th January, 2004

Dear Balbir,

We don't have a servant. I help my Mother. I get up at six o'clock. Then I sweep the rooms. Breakfast is ready at seven. I go to school at nine o'clock. In the evening I help my mother in the kitchen again. Will you write to me about yourself?

With love,

Yours sincerely,
Preeti

Now write a letter to your friend telling her about your daily routine.

Note the following points about the letter :

(1) Preeti first writes her address. She writes her house number and the name of the road. Then she writes the name of her city in the next line. Just below the name of the city writes the date.

(2) After the words Dear Balbir, Preeti puts a comma. Then she begins her letter on a new line just below the words Dear Balbir.

(3) After Preeti completes her letter she writes the words with love. Then after a comma she writes the word Yours sincerely on the next line. Then she writes her name.

➤ **14. Now read the reply given by Balbir. Balbir's letter is written below :**

302, Westened Road
Pune

17th January, 200

Dear Preeti,

Thank you for your letter.

I met with an accident last month. I was coming home on my bicycle. A car came and knocked me down. I broke my arm. I had a deep cut in my leg. I was in a hospital for two weeks. I am all right now.

Thanking You.

Yours sincerely
Balb

➤ 15. Write a letter to your friend. Congratulate her on her success.

157, Raipur Road,
Dehradun.

22nd January, 2004

Dear Nidhi,

I congratulate you on your success.

You stand first in the Quiz. You have won a month's holiday in U.K. We all are proud of you. You have worked hard to get at the top. You have brought honour to your School also. When are you flying to U.K.?

Please meet me on your return, I will like to hear all about your visit.

Yours sincerely,
Richa

➤ 16. Write a letter to a friend. Describe a match you saw yesterday.

St. Mary's School,
Carmal Road,
New Delhi.

19th January, 2004

Dear Naveen,

Your letter pleased me very much. Thank you for the same.

Yesterday, our School played a football match. The other team arrived from Sibsagar. Their Captain was very smart and active. He passed on the ball very clearly. No team could score any goal in the first half.

In the second half, our players became more active. Our captain ran with the ball. Their goal keeper came forward to meet him. Our captain slipped the ball through his legs. Thus, we scored a goal. There were only ten minutes more. The Sibsagar team tried to rush. Before the time was over, their captain also scored a goal.

Thus the match ended in a draw.

Any how, the match was very exciting. We enjoyed every minute of it.

Yours sincerely,
Dolly

➤ 17. Write a letter to a friend condoling his mother's death.

136, Civil Lines,
Allahabad.

23rd January, 2004

My dear Satish,

I am shocked to learn that your beloved mother is no more. She had, no doubt, been keeping an indifferent health for some time past, but who could have imagined that the end would come to soon. Believe me, friend, I do not find adequate words to candole you.

Your mother was a noble and pious lady. She had a heart full of affection and sympathy for others. Death has struck a severe blow. It is a personal loss to me. She regarded me as her own son. I cannot forget the love she showered on me.

But it is no use grieving. We have to gather strength to bear the misfortunes of life calmly. It is, indeed a fearful divine judgment against which we have no appeal. So it is useless to give way to despair. What can not be cured must be endured.

May God grant peace to the departed soul and give you strength to bear the loss.

In deepest sympathy.

Yours sincerely,
ABC

➤ **18. Suppose you have a friend who is a bookworm. Write a letter to him persuading him to take part in games.**

14, D.A.V. Hostel,
Imphal.

18th January, 2004

My dear Pratap,

You will not be a successful man if you remain a book-worm. You must know the world around you. I hope you know fully well saying : "All work and no play, makes jack a dull boy."

You should not shut you self in a room reading all the time. It might tell upon your health and make you unfit for the practical life. True education means proper development of body, brain and mind. If any one of these faculties is neglected, you will surely come to grief.

You must participate in games and take light exercise daiiy. It will refresh your mind and body. Recreation of the mind is necessary. There should be proper co-ordination between studies and games.

I hope you will pay attention to what I have said above.

Your sincere friend,
Atul Jain

➤ **19. Write a letter to your friend asking him to join you in a holiday visit to a few of the principal beautiful cities of India.**

25, Tagore Garden,
Jalandhar.

23rd January, 2004

My dear Pinkoo,

We are going South next month on the 15th of May, by a Deluxe Coach. We plan to visit Madras, Tirupati Temple, Setband Rameshwaram and finally spend a week in Ooty the best hill station in the South. It is on the Nilgiri Hills.

I am writing this letter in good time so that you may be able to join us on this trip. It is not only going to be very interesting but also very informative. Bring some light woollens with you for Ooty stay. For the rest only light cottons shall do.

Please let me know when I should expect you here. Remember, I won't like to have a reply in the negative. It will be a great disappointment to me if you don't come.

Do bring your camera also.

Yours sincerely,
Bikram Singh

➤ 20. Write a letter to your friend who has recovered from illness. Ask him to stay with you in your village for some time to recoup health.

Moradabad.

26th January, 2004

My dear Rakesh,

I am very happy to receive a letter in your own hand-writing. Now I believe that you have fully recovered. I have been getting letters from Anil about your illness. But this letter in your own hand-writing, has convinced me that you have fully recovered from jaundice.

I suggest that you come to my village for a few weeks. It would be a change for the better. Dear friend, I am sure you will enjoy your visit. The country side is very lovely just now and this little garden—you will certainly begin to praise it when you see the beautiful flowers—The Musk roses and the Dahlias giving out their gragrance. Close by is a stream. We often go there for fishing. You too can enjoy this sport.

Moreover, fresh air and clean water of the village will help you a lot in your weakness. I hope your father will agree to my proposal. We shall also study and discuss things. I shall myself take you out for a morning walk in open fields. I won't let you feel bored.

Please let me know when I should expect you here.

Awaiting a positive reply.

Your sincere friend,
Vishal

➤ **21. Write a letter to your friend, telling him what you intend to do after your examination.**

18, Curzon Road,
Hasimara.

23rd January, 2004

Dear Friend,

My examination is over at last. You will be glad to know that I have done pretty well. I hope to figure in the merit list. Thank God that I have come out of the ordeal of books, notes and questions.

You know I was quite nervous about his examination. So I had to put in hard work. The papers were fairly easy. I had revised almost the whole course.

Your advise to prepare all the syllabus has stood me in good stead. You have asked me what I would like to do now. I wish to join a Medical College after passing my pre-medical examination. I have a great desire to become a doctor. Our country needs a large number of well qualified doctors. Doctos command respect in society. They help in mitigating the suffering of the sick.

I hope that you will like my choice. Do drop me a line or two in reply.

Yours friendly,
ABC

➤ **22. Write a letter of apology and reconciliation to a friend with whom you have quarrelled.**

27, Model Town,
New Delhi.

29th January, 2004

My dear Anil,

It is two months since we had an unpleasant quarrel. It is no use accusing each other. I could not bear your harsh words and burst out. I am sorry and I realise my foolishness. Let us forget the past. Every one has his weakness.

My life has become listess without your warm presence. I extend to you my hand of friendship. I hope you will accept the gesture of goodwill and love. In fact it was our closeness that erupted into untold phantasy.

I am sure you will appreciate my move of reconciliation and apologise me.

Thanking you.

Yours sincerely,
XYZ

➤ **23. Write a letter to your friend telling him about your first experience in the kitchen.**

23, Sherlocks,
Kohima, Nagaland.

23rd January, 2004

My dear Subhash,

Yesterday, I was all alone in the house. What came to my mind and what did I do is indeed very interesting. so I decided so write it to you.

I thought of cooking some simple dish. Needless to mention I was very hungry. Of course it was my first day in the kitchen. I decided to cook some rice.

I poured some oil into the sauce pan and put it on the gas-stove. It became very hot and turned black in colour. I dropped some rice into it hurriedly. A few drops of oil feel on my fingers and burnt them. I forgot to pour some water. The hot oil burnt the rice completely. It was bitter when tasted. I cannot forget this awful day.

In the mean-time, my sister came from Darjeeling. She laughed and laughed. She prepared another dish of rice. She made a cup of coffee also. I was relieved of hunger.

Do write back how do you feel about my first experience in the kitchen.

Yours sincerely,
Vinay Verma

➤ **24. Write a letter to your friend who has failed in the Matriculation Examination, encouraging him to try again.**

24-K, Model Town,
Meerut.

4th January, 2004

Dear Mukesh,

I feel very sad to learn about your failure in the Matriculation Examination. It is more painful to hear that you have taken it to heart. You should know that an examination is not the real test of one's intelligence. We have been talking much about reform in the educational system. But, we have not been able to do anything in this respect.

Moreover, success and failure are the two aspects of life. You must have learnt what Lord Krishna tells Arjuna in the 'Bhagvad Gita', 'Our duty is to make efforts. The results is in the hands of God'. So, continue your efforts. You will definitely get through this time.

Your sincerely,
Rajeev

➤ 25. To a friend on his recovery from illness.

Meerut.

12th January, 2004

My dear Subodh,

It gives me great pleasure to receive the letter after a period of two months written by you. Now, I hope you are fully recovered from your long illness.

However you should take proper care during the convalescent period. You take your diet according to doctor's advice and never over strain yourself. Short walks in open air always help you recover quick.

I shall pay you visit as soon as the college is closed for Deepavali vacation.

Wishing you speedy recovery.

Your truly,
Amit Kumar

➤ 26. Write a letter to your friend congratulating him on winning a scholarship.

Thapar Nagar,
Meerut.

3rd January, 2004

My dear Ravinder,

My joy knew no bounds to learn that you have won a scholarship in the Matriculation Examination. Please accept my heartiest congratulations on your brilliant success.

It is good you have maintained your family tradition. You are in no way less intelligent than your elder brother and sister. You have brought a distinction to your school. I am very proud of having an intelligent friend like you.

Please convey my heartiest congratulations to your parents.

Yours sincerely,
Dermesh

➤ 27. To a friend congratulating him on his happy wedding.

W. K. Road,
Meerut.

9th January, 2004

My dear Subash,

Let me congratulate you most heartily upon your wedding, which marks the beginning of a new chapter in your life's career and wish you both all success and prosperity. Let every new year unite your hearts in loving affection more and more closely and bring you tidings of happiness.

May heaven bless you both with long life, health and wealth is the earnest prayer of.

Your loving friend,
Sachin Sharma

➤ 28. Write a letter to your friend describing a visit to places of historical interest.

274, Adarsh Nagar,
Meerut.

17th January, 2004

Dear Ashok,

It is only yesterday that we returned from tour. We enjoyed this tour very much.

The Taj at Agra is really a dream in marble. We visited it on the full moon. We had heard that its beauty on the moon-light-night in January is very enchanting.

From Agra, we drove to Fatehpur Sikri. It was built by Akbar. It has many historical buildings. The 'Buland Darwaja' is the most attractive. It is made of sandstone. The tomb of Saint Chisti is another beautiful monument.

I missed you very much during the tour. I wish you had been with me.

Your sincerely,
Pramod Singh

➤ 29. Write a letter to the Principal of your School. Request him to grant you leave of absence.

To,

The Principal,

Modern School,

New Delhi.

Sir,

I am suffering from fever. The doctor has advised me to take rest till Tuesday.

I regret that I cannot take the tests. I have become very weak. Kindly grant me leave of absence for seven days.

I shall be thankful to you for this kindness.

I assure you that I will make up the loss by putting in extra hours.

Yours faithfully,
Arun Sethi

➤ 30. Write an application to the Principal of your school requesting him to grant you free studentship.

To,

The Principal,

St. Thomas School,

Diphu.

Sir,

Respectfully I beg to say that I am a student of class IX of your school. My father is a mere clerk whose monthly income is Rs. 1500/-. He has a large family to support. My mother's serious illness has put the family to great financial trouble.

I, therefore, request you to grant me free studentship.

I have been a brilliant student throughout and has been enjoying full fee concession for the last five years.

I assure you, sir that I shall try my best to deserve the favour I ask of you.

Hoping that you would consider my application favourably.

Thanking you.

Your most obedient pupil,
Prem

Date : 15th January, 2004.

➤ 31. Write an application to your Principal requesting him to remit your fine. Give reasons.

To,

The Principal,

Govt. Senior Secondary School,

Bomdila.

Sir,

Most respectfully I am to say that my English teacher has fined me for not taking the special test. He thinks that I did not take the test intentionally. The fact is that I was suddenly taken ill just a day before.

As my parents were away to a marriage and there was no one in the house to deliver my application. I could not even apply for leave.

I shall feel obliged if you kindly remit the fine to Rs. 50/- imposed on me by the English teacher.

Thanking you.

Yours faithfully,
Rakesh,
Class X-A

➤ 32. Write an application to the Principal of your school, requesting him to grant you a week's leave to attend your sister's wedding.

To,

The Principal,

Holy Child School,

Bokaro.

Sir,

Most respectfully I beg to say that my sister's wedding comes off on the 10th January, 2004. As my father is alone, there is one in the house to help.

Moreover, I am the aldest son of my parents and I think it my moral duty to help them on this occasaion. I have to make arragements for food and lodging for the barat.

So I request you to grant me a week's leave to enable me to fulfil my obligation.

Thanking you.

Yours obediently,

Satish

➤ **33. Write an application to the Principal for the post of a clerk in his school.**

To,

The Principal,

D. A. V. School,

Chandigrah.

Sir,

With reference to your advertisement in 'The Hindustan Times of India' dated 27th January, 2004 for the post of a clerk in your office, I beg to offer my services for the vacancy.

As regards my educational qualifications I beg to say that I have passed my B.A. Examination in 1992. I have served as a clerk in a private firm for eight months. I also know typing. I have participated in games and sports. I have won several prizes in the debates.

I am a young man of twenty two years with good physique. If I am given a chance, I will try my best to serve your institute.

Copies of Certificates and testimonials are attached herewith for your perusal.

Thanking you.

Yours faithfully,
Vijay

➤ 34. Write an application to young Principal requesting him to exempt you from school games for a month.

To,

The Principal,
Higher Secondary School,
ABC City.

Sir,

With due respect, I beg to state that I sprained my right ankle on Sunday last while playing basket ball. I got it examined a Indian Institute of Medical Sciences, New Delhi. Its X-ray photograph reveals that there is a compound fracture in the bone also.

The doctor has advised me to take complete rest for a month. I shall be taking some medicines also. I have been asked to desist from taking part in games for some time.

I, therefore, request you to exempt me from school games for about a month and obliged.

Yours obediently,
K. S. Minhas,
Class 10th C

Date : 27th January, 2004

➤ **35. There is an advertisement for the post of typist in a newspaper. Apply for the post giving your biodata.**

Kanpur.

27th January, 2004

To,

The Managar,

MCS Ltd.

Park Street, Calcutta.

Sub : Application for the post of a typist.

Sir,

With reference to your advertisement for the job of typist in **'THE HINDU'** dated 15th January, 2004 I beg to offer my services for the same.

My biodata is an under :

BIO-DATA

Name	:	Rakesh Kumar
Father's Name	:	S. K. Gupta
Age	:	19 years
Eduational	:	Passed B. Com. Exam. in
Qualifications	:	1992 in Ist Div.

Speed in typewriting	:	40 words per minute
Experience	:	Worked as typist to the District Inspector of Schools in a 6 month's leave vacancy.

During my school and college career I took active part in all the literary and social activities of the Institutions in which I studied. I also worked as the Editor of the College Magazine.

I attach herewith true copies of my testimonials for your perusual.

I beg to request you to give me an opportunity to serve your organisation.

Assuring you a sincere and devoted service.

Thanking you.

Yours faithfully,
Rakesh Kumar,
15, Civil Lines, Kanpur.

➤ **36. Write a letter to the Chairman of your municipality, complaining of the insanitary condition of the locality in which you live and asking him to take necessary steps in the matter. (Do not write your name)**

To,

The Mayor,

Guwahati Municipal Corporation,

Guwahati.

Subject : Insanitary condition of the "Vikas Nagar"

Dear Sir,

I beg to draw your kind attention to the insanitary condition of my locality. The people of Vikas Nagar are feeling miserable.

There is no sewage system in this area. Gutters are open.

Often the dirty waters is flowing on the roads and lanes. The heaps of dirt and garbage lying here and there have not been removed for weeks. Rain water collects in them and mosquitoes breed there in large numbers.

If immediate attention is not paid to improve the situation, some epidemic may break out soon.

I, therefore, request you to take effective steps to improve the insanitary condition in the locality. There is no need to remind you that it is the duty of your department to look after the health and hygiene of the people and the area.

Expecting a prompt action.

Yours faithfully,
ABC

➤ **37. Write a letter in about 100 words to the Superintendent of Police, reporting the theft of your bicycle.**

18, DLF Colony,
Guwahati.

23rd January, 2004

To,

The Superintendent of Police,
Kamrup District,
Guwahati.

Sir,

I beg to report the theft of my cycle today. This morning I went to the State Bank of India. A. T. Road, Guwahati at about 11 A.M. I placed my cycle near the main gate. I locked it properly. I got a cheque cashed and came out of the bank. To my surprise, I found my bicycle missing. I enquired from many persons but none could give any clue.

It's make is Atlas. It bears No. 2506. It is quite a new bicycle. I bought it form the C.S.D. recently.

Kindly look into the matter at your earliest.

Yours faithfully,
Ram Dass

➤ 38. Write a letter to the Editor of a newspaper complaining of the frequent breakdown of electricity in your locality.

L-15, Model Town,
New Delhi.

1st January, 2004

To,

The Editor,

The Times of India,

New Delhi.

Sir,

Through the columns of your esteemed daily, I wish to express my concern about frequent breakdown in our locality.

The condition of power supply in our locality is indeed, very disappointing. The supply breaksdown very frequently and at odd times, mid-night or the after-noon. This results in misery to children and old people. Fans, coolers and refrigerators become useless during these hot days.

This matter has been brought to the notice of the S.D.O. Electricity many a time but to no avial.

I request you to publish this grievance so that the authorities concerned realize the difficulty and look into the problem and do the needful.

Thanking you.

Yours truly,
Vivek Arora

➤ 39. Write a letter to the Transport Manager of your city informing him that there are insufficient buses on your route in the morning.

105, Defence Colony,
New Delhi.

1st January, 2004

To,

The Manager,

Delhi Transport Corporation,

New Delhi.

Dear Sir,

It is to bring to your kind notice that the buses plying on outer Ring Road to West Pate Nagar are insufficient.

The office-geers, students and other workers have to wait for half an hour to get a bus. The buses coming from Lajpat Nagar are packed to their capacity. Moreover, they do not stop at Patel Nagar bus-stop. We are, therefore, suffering a lot.

I, therefore, request you to introduce some more buses on this route.

Thanking you.

Yours sincerely,
Vikas Jain

➤ **40. Write a letter to the Director, Delhi Doordarshan telling him about some of T.V. Programmes (1) you enjoy (2) you dislike (3) you would like to be introduced.**

131, West Patel Nagar,
New Delhi.

12th January, 2004

To,

The Director,

Delhi Doordarshan,

New Delhi.

Dear Sir,

I have the honour to share some of my views with you about your programmes. It is a matter of great satisfaction that the Delhi Doordarshan has introduced some novel programmes like "Parakh" and "Janadesh".

The programmes on Sports and Science are also a welcome change. But your programme on classical music needs better handling. So is the one on Yoga and Agriculture. They lack natural touch. The Metro Channel has swayed the audience.

But the selection of feature films is not very good. You should select quality films may be of any language.

Please introduce some more programmes like "The Discovery of India".

Thanking you.

Yours faithfully,
Vinay Gupta

➤ 41. Write a letter to the Editor of a National daily expressing your views about Environmental pollution and its remedies.

23, Tagore Garden,
Baramulla,
Srinagar.

26th January, 2004

The Editor,
The North East Times,
Guwahati.

Sub : Threat of Pollution.

Sir,

Kindly allow me to express my views on the problem of Environmental pollution through the esteemed columns of your daily.

Today, Environmental pollution has become a matter of serious concern the world over.

Unfortunately men in his greed for material advancement has so far been destroying his very benefactors.

Fumes on the ever increasing number of vehicles on our roads have led to a situation of grave danger to health.

People and the Govt. has become fully alert. Various steps have been initiated in this direction.

More attention is being paid to afforestation. Scientists have been asked to find out ways and means of curbing the menance of smoke. Stringent punishment should be meted out to the defaulters. The supervisory machinery should be geered up.

Of course, Environmental awareness is a social responsibility. Mere Government efforts can not yield much desired results. The need is to educate the people. To maintain a pollution free environment should be the prime concern of each and every individual today.

Your faithfully,
Uma Bhargava

➤ **42. Write a letter to your land-lord asking him to get certain repairs done in the house you are occupying.**

F-21, South Extension,
New Delhi.

10th January, 2004

Dear Sir,

I am writing this letter to draw your attention to the repairs which the house, urgently needs.

During the recent rains, the roof of the house leaked badly. The water which trickled down through the ceiling has spoiled our costly furniture. The doors and windows need repainting. The plaster has come off at many places.

I shall feel obliged if you carry out the necessary repair in the house at the earliest.

Please treat it as very urgent.

Yours faithfully,
B. R. Khanna.

➤ **43. You have been given the name and address of a person of your age group living in some foreign country who is interesting in making pen friends. Write your first letter to him on her about yourself, giving your personal appearance, interests, hobbies etc.**

J. Turner
40-Oxford Street,
Manchester (U.K.).

B-724 Saket, Meerut
20th January, 2004

Dear J. Turner,

I have learnt through the column of the "Readers Digest" that you are interested in making friendship with Indian boys. Having read your particulars, I feel that we can become very good friends.

We belong to same age group. I am a young boy of Sixteen. I study in class XI. I belong to a respectable family. My father is an army officer and my mother is a doctor.

I am interested in playing cricket and have been the captain of the school. Gardening and photography are my hobbies.

I hope you will give detailed account of your likings and hobbies. I am very eagar to hear from you

Yours sincerely,
Ajay Kumar

➤ **44. You are Secretary of your School Literary Society. Write a letter to the Editor Daily News, New Delhi, requesting him to address one of the weekly meetings of your society.**

Falcon Society,
Modern School,
Janakpuri, New Delhi.

30th January, 2004

To,

The Editor,

Daily News.

Sir,

We propose to hold inaugural function of our Falcon Society of our school in first week of July.

As secretary of the society, I have been asked to invite some eminent person to address the members of the Society. I request you kindly to give your learned talk to members of the society.

I hope you would kindly accept to our request and intimate time and date convenient to you in advance.

Thanking you.

Yours faithfully,

sd/- ABC
(Secretary)

➤ **45. Write a letter to a sports goods or manufacturer to send you some sports material.**

25, Krishna Nagar,
New Delhi.

18th January, 2004

To,

M/s Champion Sports,
Suraj Kund Road,
Meerut.

Dear Sir,

Kindly supply the following articles of sports per passenger train at your earliest convenience. The R/R may be sent through the State Bank of India, Krishna Nagar, New Delhi. Good should be carefully packed in a wooden box and then covered with gunny bag.

(1)	Badminton Racquet Steel Shaft	De-luxe Brand	10 pcs.
(2)	Badminton Nets Cotton	Parrot Brand	2 pcs.
(3)	Shuttle-Cocks	Queen Brand	10 dozen
(4)	Volleyball laceless	Tiger Brand	6 pcs.
(5)	Cricket Bats		6 pcs.

Thanking you,

Yours faithfully,
Rakesh Sharma

➤ **46. Write a letter to the Manager of a local mill seeking his permission to visit to the mill.**

To,

The General Manager,
Delhi Cloth Mills,
Delhi.

Dear sir,

We shall feel much obliged if you very kindly allow a batch of fifty students of this school to visit your Mills on the coming Saturday.

I may, however assure you that our students would go round the factory in a well-disciplined manner. Our senior teachers would escort them. You will, however, not find any sort of disorder.

Besides it will be a good opportunity for us to meet you.

We shall feel much obliged if you very kindly depute one of your officials to show us round the Mills.

Thanking you in anticipation.

Yours faithfully,
Vipin Sharma
Falcon Club
St. Mary's Acadamy,
Shillong.

➤ 47. Write a letter to a foreigner describing how a wedding is conducted in India.

H-3, Shastri Nagar,
Meerut.

24th January, 2004

Dear Mr. Harry,

In your last letter, you have asked me to tell you how weddings are performed in India. As per your desire, I am describing an Indian wedding. The engagement ceremony is conducted by the parents of the boy and the girl, of course both of them are asked their choice. The parents of the bride and bridegroom settle the date by mutual consent.

On the fixed date, the bridegroom dressed in his best, rides on a mare and reached the bride's house. He gives a princely look. At the brideg's place, the bride, dressed in red, garlands the bridegroom.

The youngmen, women, girls and children dance to the romantic tunes of the band. The marriage party gets a grand reception, with drinks and dinner.

The bridge and the bridegroom are made to sit on a raised dias for the performance of rituals. The pandits chant the vedic hymns and the marital rituals are performed. The girl is given rich presents, jewellery, clothes and numerous valuables as dowry.

Then, it is the time for the bride to take leave to her parents. It is a moving time for her and her family. The bride goes to the bridegroom's house.

Yours sincerely,
Akash Jain

❑❑❑

SHORT STORIES

SHORT-STORIES

Introduction

The Origin of Story telling can be traced back, perhaps to those of our cave dwelling ancestors. We have stories of various kinds from unknown part. Stories such as folk and *puranic* nature are part of the culture of that land; Fancy tales of any language and place provide joy to all of us; Fables teach moral and wisdom of humankind.

Our country reaches the piracle in the art of story telling thousand of years back. The stories of 'Panchatantra-Hitopadesa', 'Jataka tales' and tales from 'Katha Sarit Sagara' of Gunadhya are famous, permanent and examplary very little is known of Aesop but his fable are well-known throughout the world. The lessons of love, wisdom and mercy taught by these stories to human beings are as true and applicable as they were centuries back.

Here stories from Aesops fables, Panchatantra and some folk tales were taken to teach the art of story writing.

A story can be developed by knowing :

(a) detailed outline,

(b) a sketchy outline,

(c) well known proverbs.

A story can also be developed through imagination or otherwise knowledge.

Hints for writing a Good Story

(i) Careful reading of the outline.

(ii) Filling the missing sequences by imagination.

(iii) Completion of the story by connecting the various points gathered in a most natural way.

(iv) The story can be made juicy or spicy by introducing dialogues at appropriate places.

(v) A good story possess descriptive introduction, fast movement of idea in the middle portion and a twist in the conclusion.

(vi) Heading or title of the story should indicate either the main characters, theme incident or proverb or a well-known quotation.

(vii) Use of correct and simple idiomatic English is a must for writing a good story.

THE HARE AND THE TORTOISE

Once a hare met a tortoise near a pool of water. They became friends and spent a lot of time together. Whenever, they met, the hare made fun of the tortoises small feet and slow pace. The tortoise was very pleasant. He bore the insults gently.

A day came when the tortoise could not bear the insult any more. He challenged the hare to have a race with him. The hare accepted the challenge.

They were to start recovery from the pool the next morning and it was decided that who reached the bridge earlies which was two miles away, would be declared the winner. The race started next morning. They was soon out of right. The tortoise moved slowly. On the way the hare lay down to have a nap under a shady tree. Soon he fell asleep.

The tortoise all this time moved on slowly but steadily. It reached the bridge before the hare to welcome him with these words :

"Slow and steady wins the race".

KING BRUCE AND THE SPIDER OR NEVER LOSE HEART

Many centuries ago there lived a king in Scotland The king's name was Robert Bruce. He was noble and brave king. He loved his country very much. He wanted to free Scotland from yoke of the British. England and Scotland were, therefore, constantly at war.

Robert Bruce gathered a big army and fought against the English six times. But every time he was defeated. He had a narrow escape. His sixth defeat broke his heart. He retired into the forest. He hid in a dark cave and was so disgusted that he thought of ending of life with a dagger.

Suddenly his eyes fell upon a spider. It was trying to reach the ceiling. It fell down on the floor. After a short while, it tried again. But it fell down once again. Every time it fell, it started climbing all over again.

At last it was successful in its attempt to reach the roof. The sight enthused him to try again. The spider had taught him a lesson "Never say die" But try, Try again". He again gathered a big army and defeated the English.

THE CAPSELLER AND THE MONKEYS

A Capseller was returning from a village-fair. He had made a big-profit there. He was happy. He had with him ten red caps left unsold. The sun was blazing hot. He felt tired and hungry. He sat under a shady tree on the way side. He drew water from a nearby well. He had his lunch and lay down for a nap and soon feel asleep. The bundle of unsold caps lay near him.

As the capseller was enjoying sound sleep, a monkey climbed down the tree and took away the bundle of caps. The monkeys found nothing to eat in the bundle of caps. They put on the caps on their head.

When the capseller woke up he found his bundle of caps missing. He could see no one around who might have stolen his caps. As he looks up he saw the monkeys wearing the caps. He throws pebbles at monkeys but they climbed up higher.

He cursed the monkeys. He threw away the cap was wearing, in disgust. The monkeys, in imitation of the capseller, did the same. In this way, the capseller got all his caps back.

THE SHEPHERD BOY AND THE WOLF OR THINK TWICE BEFORE YOU ACT

A village boy was employed to keep a watch on the flock of sheep. He used to take sheep out for grazing on the hill side. Being alone the whole day, he felt bored. He decided to play a trick.

He started shouting. A Wolf ! The villager heared his cries and rushed to his help. On reaching there, they found the boy laughing at them. There was not wolf. They scolded the boy and returned to the village.

After a week the mischievous boy played the same joke again. The villagers hastened to his help with sticks once again there was no wolf. Their eyes rolled with anger and they gave the boy a good beating.

The very next day, a wolf, really came there. The boy saw the animal from a distance. He was terribly frightened. He began to shout at the top of his voice. The villagers did not believe him, so they paid no heed to his cry for help. The wolf pounced upon the boy and killed him.

THE ASS AND HIS LOAD OF SALT OR ONE SHOULD NOT BE OVER CLEVER

Once there lived a merchant in a village. He had a clever ass. The merchant brought goods from the city on its back. One day the merchant was bringing salt from the city. A stream lay on the way. When the ass entered the stream its foot slipped and the bag fell into the stream. The salt dissolved in the water. The load became lighter. The ass was very happy.

The next day the merchant again brought salt. This time the ass fell down in the stream knowingly and much of the salt was dissolved in water. The merchant saw through the donkey's trick and decided to teach him a lesson.

Next day he loaded the ass with cotton. As usual, the ass lay down in the mid-stream. He had hoped that burden would gross less. But to the surprise of the ass, the burden increased this time. It could hardly move but the merchant beat it with his stick.

TWO FRIENDS AND THE BEAR

Once two friends were going on a long journey. On their way, they had to pass through a dense wood. They promised to help each other on the way. In those days there were no transport. They had to walk through forest, full of dangerous wild animals. When they were passing through the forest, they saw a bear running towards them. One of them knew how to climb the tree. He went up the tree in no time. The other was poor at climbing. He could not find any way to save himself. At last he threw himself on the ground and lay there motionless. When the bear came near him he stopped breathing. The bear sniffed him. He took him for a dead man and went away.

When the bear had gone. The friend on the tree came down. He asked his friend who was lying on the ground "What did the bear say in your ear? The letter remembered his friend not coming to his rescue. He replied that the bear had said to him, "Never trust a selfish friend".

HALF THE PROFITS OR HONESTY IS THE BEST POLICY

A king was holding a grand feast in his palace. He needed fish for it. A fisherman brought a nice fish for the king. But the gate keeper did not allow him. He demanded half the profit which the fisherman would get. The fisherman agreed to share the reward with him.

The king was very glad to see the big fish and asked the fisherman the price of fish. The fisherman replied. On hundred lashes on my back. The people present there were surprised to hear such a strange price. The king offered the fisherman gold coins. But the fisherman insisted that he be lashed on the back. At last the king ordered the lashes to be given on his bare back.

After receving fifty lashes on his back, the fisherman said, Stop Stop ! I have another partner in business. He is gate keeper. He wanted half of what I get. The king at once called the gate-keeper. The man was given fifty hand lashes. He punished the gate-keeper. And the fisherman was rewarded suitably for his wit.

THREE GREEDY FRIENDS

Once there lived three friends in a village. One day they decided to go to a city to earn their living. They promised to help each other in case of any trouble.

On their way, they passed through a thick forest. In the forest, they found a leather bag which was full of gold coins. They were very happy. They decided to divide the coins in three equal parts. They sat down under a tree. By then they felt hungry. One person was sent to buy some food and wine, while the other two stayed behind.

The two friends, who stayed behind decided to kill the third friend so that they might have his share for themselves. Mean while, the third friend decided to kill the other two so that he might have all the gold coins. He mixed some poison in the food and returned. The other two killed him as soon as he reached the place. Now the two friend were happy and ate the food. They too died on the spot.

Hence the life of the three greedy friends came to an end.

THE SLAVE AND THE LION

The king of a certain country had half a dozen slaves. He treated them harshly. One evening a young slave ran away from his palace. He escaped into the forest infested with wild animals. Outside a cave, he saw a lion crying in pain. Perhaps it had run into a thorny bush. The beast growled furiously. He pulled out the thorn from the lion's paw. For a few days it limped. The wound healed and it was all right.

A few months later the slave was caught. The king decreed. That the slave be thrown before a hungry lion. It was the severest punishment ever awarded to any offender. The poor slave was helpless. He was pushed into a lion's cage. The hungry lion roared and leapt from his place.

But it stoped short and began to lick the slave's feet. It recognised the man and remembered his kindness. It was the same fellow who had once taken out the thorn from his paw. The people watched this scene in great amazment. The moral of the story is Goodnees neveer goes unrewarded.

A WISE JACKAL OR A BRAHMIN AND THE JACKAL

Once there was a poor Brahmin. While travelling across a forest he saw a tiger caught up in a trap. He took pity upon the tiger and released from the cage by opening its door.

The tiger was very hungry. After coming out of the cage the tiger wanted to eat the poor Brahmin. He was in a fix. He regretted having done a good turn to the tiger. He pleaded the tiger to spare his life as he had saved him from the imprisonment. He proposed that they should ask some one else. So they went to a peepal tree.

The Brahmin thought that the peepal would its opinion in his favour because he had often worshipped it. But the Peepal said that all the men were selfish and ungrateful. It gave them shade but still they cut its branches.

Then they went to a bullock. He told the tiger to eat the Brahmin because his master beat him and did not feed him well. Hearing this, the Brahmin was dejected. Just then, a Jackal happened to pass that way. He was very wise. He saw through the wickedness of the tiger. So he said that he would decide the matter after he had actually seen how it had happened.

So the tiger, the Brahmin and the Jackal came to that place. The cage was still lying there. He asked the tiger to show him how he was caught in the cage. The tiger jumped into the cage. The Jackal asked the Brahmin to shut the door. Then he asked the Brahmin to go away. The tiger was once again in the cage.

We should not forget the good done by others to us.

BELLING THE CAT OR IT IS EASY TO SAY BUT DIFFICULT TO DO

There lived some mice in a village. There was a big cat. All the mice were scared of the cat. Each day, some one was attacked and eaten away by the cat. Their number became less and less. They were upset.

They called a meeting of all the mice to discuss the threat of the cat. There were many suggestions. At last, they decided that they should bell the cat to signal her arrival. Everybody accepted the proposal. They were happy, but an old mice stood up and asked : who will bell the cat?

All were struck up with silence. No one was ready to risk its life to bell the cat. In the meantime, the cat came there. The mice were mice after all. They all ran away in to their holes.

VIRTUE IS ALWAYS HONOURED OR THE MOUSE AND THE LION

There was a lion in a forest. Once it lay asleep under the shade of a tree. A mouse lived nearby. When the lion was asleep the mouse climbed over its body and began to jump and play.

In the meantime, the lion woke up. He was surprised to see the mouse on his body. Immediately the lion caught the mouse in his paws. The mouse got terrified. It pleaded the lion to forgive it this time. It promised to help him in distress. The lion was noble hearted. He was impressed at the appeal of mercy of the mouse. So he let the mouse go unharmed.

A few days later, a hunter came to the forest. He laid a snare. The lion was caught in to it. Now the lion was in trouble. It roared in agony. The mouse heared the roar. He remembered his word of promise to help the lion in need. He rushed there to rescue the lion.

It cut the strings of the net with its teeth and thus the lion got free. He thanked the mouse very much.

We should never consider others small or insignificant.

A GREEDY DOG

There lived a dog in a certain town. One day, he got a piece of meat. He was very selfish and greedy. He wanted to eat that piece of meat all alone. So he came out of the town to its outskirts. There was a stream on the way. As he crossed the river from the bridge, he saw his reflection in the water of the stream.

Being greedy, he thought that there was another dog with a piece of meat. He wanted to get that piece of meat also from him. So he barked to scare the other dog.

As he opened his mouth, his own piece of meat fell in the stream. Thus he lost what he had in the greed for more.

The story teaches us a moral that we should not be greedy.

A THIRSTY CROW OR "WHERE THERE IS A WILL, THERE IS A WAY"

There was a crow in a village. He was very clever. One hot day, he felt very thirsty. That year, there were no rains. All the rivers and the ponds had gone dry. He flew here and there in search of water.

He saw a pitcher of water in a garden. He was overjoyed. But it when began to drink water. He found that the level of water in the pitcher was very low. His beak could not reach it. He felt unhappy. He thought and thought for some time. Then he collected some pebbles. He threw them one by one in the pitcher. The water rose up in level.

He quenched his thirst and flew away happily thinking that nothing is impossible in this world.

A FOX AND THE GRAPES

Once there was a clever fox. One day, he felt hungry. He went about in search of some food in the forest. He reached an orchard of grapes. Fine, round and ripe grapes were hanging from their vines. They were a visual feast.

He was overjoyed to see them. He wanted to eat them at once. So he jumped. But the vines were too high for him to reach. He jumped many times. But he did not succeed in getting at the grapes. He got tired and left the idea of eating grapes in disgust. But he did not accept defeat. He went away saying that the grapes were sour. So it was good that he did not eat them.

Obviously what else he could do to console himself.

GOD HELPS THOSE WHO HELP THEMSELVES

There was a cartman. One rainy day, he was driving his cart on a muddy road. One of the wheels got stuck up in a mud hole. He tried and tried. He even beat up his bullocks but the cart could not be pulled out. He got disappointed and helpless.

Then he thought of God Herculus. He prayed to him for help. His prayer was sincere and true. So the God appeared there in person. He advised the cartman not to lose heart. He asked him to put his shoulder to wheel. As the cartman did so, the cart moved out of the mud.

The bullocks heaved a sign of relief. He was equally happy. The God disappeared. But he had taught the cartman that God helps those who help themselves.

The moral of the story is trust your hands and put them to work.

A BEE AND THE DOVE OR A GOOD TURN DESERVES ANOTHER

A good turn deserves another. There was a busy bee. Once it fell into a pond of water. A swift current of water drove it along. A dove was sitting on a tree close by. It saw the miserable plight of the bee.

Immediately it got up to help her. It plucked leaf and threw it near the bee. The bee lost no time. As it saw the leaf, it climbed on it. It thanked the dove for saving its life.

Time passed. One day the same dove was sitting on a tree. A hunter came there. He was taking aim at the dove with his gun. The bee saw this. It sensed the danger and stung the hunter. He cried in pain and missed the shot. The gun dropped from his hand. The dove flew away. It knew the bee had saved its life and repaid the earlier act of goodness.

A VAIN STAG OR PRIDE HATH A FALL

There lived a stag in acertain forest. One day he felt thirsty. He went to a nearby pond. As he bent to take water, he saw his reflection in the clean water of the pond. He swelled up at the beauty of his horns. But when he saw his legs, he began to curse God.

As he stood cursing, there was a heavy barking of hounds in the distance. He turned to see the approaching dogs. He saw them and ran hard. His ugly legs carried him to a considerable distance. But when he tried to hide himself in the bushes its beautiful horns got stuck up. The hounds came near and pounced upon him. They killed him.

Now who can understand the mysteries of God. Ugly legs had tried to save him while the beautiful horns had brought about his death.

UNION IS STRENGTH

Once there was an old father. He had three sons. They did not love one another. Their father was upset. He often advised them to live peace and not to quarrel. But they were very obstinate.

One day the old man got sick. He lay on his death bed. He was worried about his sons. He called them and asked them to bring a bundle of sticks. They immediately obeyed him an brought a bundle.

Then he aksed them one by one to try to break the bundle. None of them could do so. He asked them to untie the bundle. There after he asked them to break all sticks. All the three could easily break the sticks.

The sons understood the message. So long as the sticks were tied together, they could not break them. So if they lived untidely, nobody will be able to harm them.

They followed their old father's advice and learnt that union is strength.

THE WIND AND THE SUN

Once there was a quarrel between the wind and sun. Each claimed itself to be stronger than the other. They ventured to exhibit their power on a man coming from some distance.

First, it was wind's turn to exhibits its strength. It began to blow hard. It wanted to blow off his coat. But the harder it blew, the more closer did the man hold his coat to his body. It tried and tried to make the man remove his coat. But it failed.

Now it was the turn of the sun. It began to shine brightly and grew in its intensity. The man felt warm. He could not bear the growing heat so he unbuttoned his coat. It was still very hot. At last he took off his coat. The sun smiled. It has won. Thereafter the wind never took airs.

AN ELEPHANT AND THE TAILOR OR TIT FOR TAT

Once there was an elephant called Rammana. It used to go to a river to take a bath. On his way to the river, there was a tailor. The elephant used to put its trunk in the shop. The tailor used to give him some eatable. This continued for some time. Soon they became friends.

One day, the tailor was unwell. He was also mentally upset. As usual the elephant came on its way. He thrust inside the shop expecting some food. But to his surprise and shock, the tailor pricked a needle into his trunk. The elephant felt hurt. It decided to take it out on the tailor.

At the river, it took its bath and then took some muddy water in its trunk. On way back, it again passed the tailor's shop. "Now was the time to take revenge" he thought. And he released the muddy water into the shop there by spoiling new clothes. The tailor suffered a great loss. He had to pay dearly for his rash action.

A BLIND MAN WHO CARRIED A LAMP OR DO GOOD

Once there was an old man in a village. He was blind. But he was gentle and polite. He was self reliant. He never took unnecessary help from others.

After sunset, he used to carry a lamp. The village boys often laughed at him. They called him an idiot and a fool.

They wondered why did he carry a lamp when he can't see but the blind man was not short tempered. He did not get angry. He told them "Look boys. Agreed that I can't see but I carry if for others to see me." The village boys felt ashamed of their unbecoming conduct. They apologised to him for their folly. There after they never made fun of the old and blind man.

THE CUNNING WOLF

Once there was a wolf in a forest. He was very cunning. One day it caught a rabbit. While eating it, a sharp bone got stuck up in his throat.

Now he was in trouble. He couldn't eat anything. Besides, there was pain. So he went to his friend animals for help. But no one was ready to help him as they were afraid of him.

At last, a crane took pity on him and agreed to take out the bone his throat with its sharp beak. But when the crane asked for the reward, the wolf became furious. "You silly creature. What reward do you want? I allowed your beak in my throat and did not bite it."

The crane knew that the wolf shall always be wolf. Better forget about the reward.

TWO CATS AND A MONKEY OR NEVER QUARREL OVER A TRIFLE

There were two fat cats. One of them was black and the other was white. One day, they found a piece of cake. They started quarelling about who shall take the bigger share. The white cat said it had seen the cake so it should be her privilage to have a bigger share. The black cat thought and believed the other way round.

In the meantime, a monkey came there. He ventured to settle their quarrel. He said that he would divide the cake into two equal parts. The cats agreed. So he brought a pair of scales and set to divide the cake.

The monkey broke the cake into two pieces. Then he put one piece in each pan. On lifting the scales, he found that one piece weighed heavier than the other. So he took a bite from the heavier one and ate it up. But look now the other piece became heavier. So he took a bite from the second piece to make it equal to the first one. The process continued.

At last the cats were shocked to notice that the pieces had become very small and still the monkey continued to eat one after the other. They saw his trick and asked him to stop dividing the cake any further.

They asked the monkey to give them those small pieces. But the monkey refused saying that it was the reward for his labour. And he put those small pieces in his mouth. The cats had lost the entire cake. Now they realised that contentment is a virtue.

THE CATE AND THE FOX

Once there lived a fox and a cat in a jungle. They always used to boast about his greatness and cleverness. One day the fox told the cat 'You know I am very clever. I know hundreds of tricks so my enemies can not catch me'. For this the cat smiled and said 'I know only one way'.

Just then they heard the loud barks of hunting dogs and saw some men. The cat quickly climbed up the tree and hid in the branches. The fox began to think. He could not decide the way of escape. It was too late. The dogs and men caught and killed the fox.

THE HARE AND THE LION OR MENTAL STRENGTH IS SUPERIOR TO MUSCLE STRENGTH

Once there lived a huge lion in a thick forest. He was very cruel. He killed animals indiscriminately. All the other animals of the forest were very much afraid of this cruel lion.

One day they all gathered together to find out a plan to get rid of such a lion. Even after a lengthy discussion they could not find any satisfactory solution to the problem. The leader of the gathering addressed the animals assembled. 'Is there any body who can get rid of this cruel lion'? To this a small hare got up and said 'I can kill the lion'. Hearing this all the assembled animals then laughed and laughed.

The hare once more said in a firm tone and in all seriousness. 'Now leave the problem, of the lion to me, I have a plan. I will be able to kill him by the coming full moon day'. Then the leader dispersed the assembly.

The hare hatched a plan. To execute that plan, on the full moon day the hare went straight to the lion's den. There the hare saw the fierce lion. The lion roared with anger. 'Why do you come hare? Do you want to die in my hands right now'? To this the hare replied humbly, 'Salutations! to you, the king of the forest. I came here with a message from a very big lion which challenges your highness to a combat'. The lion roared back. 'I am the mighty king who ruled this forest. I do not want any rival. Show me where he lives. I will fight and kill him'.

The hare took him to a deep well which was on the out skirts of the forest, according to the plan. The hare said to the lion, 'Sir! the new lion lived inside the well'. The lion looked inside the well. He saw his own reflection in the deep waters of the well in the full-moon light. He roared into the well against his own reflection. And his image roared back with resounding voice. The lion became furious and jumped into the well to fight with the image. Alas! he lost his own life. Thus the clever hare put the lion to death.

All the other animals came to know the whole episode and felt happy. They rejoiced the death of the cruel lion and praised the cleverness of the hare.

THE WOLF AND THE LAMB

There was a village on the out skirts of a forest. In that village a shepherd lived in the small hut with a flock of sheep. A lamb strayed away from the flock to drink water in a brook. A wolf also came to drink water in the brook. He saw the lamb and decided to eat the lamb. But felt he had to find a pretext to kill.

So the wolf said to the lamb in anger. "Why are you dirtying up my water?" The lamb said meekly. "I am sorry sir! but I am drinking water in the down stream so how can I dirty the water? To this reply the wolf angrily shouted "Do you not know how to respect elders? Last year also you abused me like this, you should be punished for your imprudence".

The lamb said with shivering voice, "But sir! I was not born last year and I am only six months old".

"Then", the wolf said "It must have been your father, you must pay the price for his folly". So saying the wolf and jumped on the lamb and ate.

THE CRANE AND THE FOX

There was a lake in a dense forest. By the side of the lake there were many big trees. A crane lived on the trees and ate fish in the lake. Also there is a clever fox which lived in the forest. The crane some times shared with the fox the fish it caught in the lake. The both became good friends.

The fox one day thought he would play a joke on his friend. So he said to the crane, "Will you come to dine with me"? The crane replied, 'Yes friend! I shall come".

When the crane arrived the fox welcomed the bird warmly. But when they sat to dine, the fox served soup only that too in flat plates.

The fox was able to lap up the whole soup with his tongue easily. But the crane on account of his long bill was not able to drink the soup from the flate plate. The fox had filled his stomach. He also laughed at the crane for its inability to drink. The crane even though hungry did not show her discomfort. The crane thought "I shall teach the fox a lesson". So one day he said to the fox, "Dear friend, will you please come to dine with me"? The fox readily agreed to come.

At the dinner the crane also served just soup but in two jugs of long and narrow necks. The crane was able to put the long bill into the jug and drink happily. The fox was not able to drink at all. But licked the jug only from outside. The fox remained hungry. Now it was the crane's turn to laugh at the fox. The fox realised the mistake he committed and cooly went away.

THE LION AND THE MOUSE

Once upon a time huge lion ruled the forest. All the animals were afraid of him.

One day after a good hunt the lion lept under a tree. A little mouse from the near by hole moved over the lion and disturbed his sleep.

The lion woke up and was very angry. He caught the mouse in his big paw and said "You tiny rascal, you have awakened me I shall now kill you". The mouse shook with fear and said to the lion. "You are the king of the forest, I am a little mouse. Please do not kill me. Perhaps I may help you if you save me now". To this the lion laughed and said, "Your tiny creature! How will you help me"? However he let the mouse go free from his paw.

After few days some hunters laid a trap to catch the lion. The lion trapped in the net. The lion roared and roared but could not come out of the net.

The little mouse heard the roar of the lion. It saw the same lion caught in the net and helpless. The mouse at once began to cut the strings of the net. Soon the lion was set free from the trap.

The lion thanked the mouse for its timely help.

THE DOVE AND THE ANT

In a forest there lived a dove on a tree top by the side of stream. Near the tree there was an ant hill. One day an ant crowled away and fell into the flowing stream. The ant was in great danger. The dove on the tree saw it. The bird dropped a twig near the ant. The ant climbed on the twig.

Soon the twig reached the bank drived by wind. The ant came on the land and was saved.

Some days after a fowler came into the forest. He aimed an arrow at the dove. The fowler was about to release the arrow from his bow. The ant saw the danger to the dove. It came near the fowler and stung deep in his foot. The fowler jerked his foot and lost the aim. The dove flew away unharmed. The life of the dove was saved by the ant.

THE HEN THAT LAID GOLDEN EGGS

Long time back there lived a poor peasant in a small village along with his family. They were very poor. Both wife and sons worked along with him in the fields for their living.

One day they found a beautiful chick of golden colour lying before their hut. The chick was hurt and wounded. They nursed and cared the chick. In due course of time the chick turned into a beautiful hen of golden feathers. The hen was quite different from ordinary fowls.

After some days the hen laid an egg. To their surprise they found the egg was of pure gold. They were very happy. They were much pleased with the hen. All the villagers looked at the wonderful hen with respect.

The wonderful hen laid one golden egg every day in the morning. Now their poverty disappeared. They purchased lot of land and a beautiful house.

The peasant and his wife became greedy. They thought if the hen will die there will be no more golden eggs and also getting one egg a day is a slow process. Hence they wanted to cut the stomach of the hen to take out all the golden eggs at once.

The foolish and greedy couple caught hold of the hen and cut the stomach. To their disappointment they found nothing except flesh and blood like any other hen.

The peasant and his wife were very sad and unhappy. They paid a heavy price for their greed.

THE BIRD COUPLE AND THE FOOLISH MONKEYS

To advise a brute is to dig once own grave. It was a winter night. Deep inside the jungle the cold was very severe. On such a cold winter night a group of monkeys were thinking aloud with shivering bodies "What to do to get warmth". One monkey said "Make fire". "The red fire and flame gives lot of warmth". All the monkeys were happy and appreciated the monkey for his good suggestion.

To make fire they gathered dry twigs and that fell under the trees into a heap. "To lit the fire, what should we do"? The monkey questioned themselves. Once more they all negotiated with each other. This time another monkey said "Why to worry when there are lot of fire flies all around us." This idea was greeted with applause. All the monkeys praised this one also for his intelligence.

In no time they collected about a handful of glow warms. They put all these glow warms amongst the heap of twigs they collected and started blowing air with their mouth to make fire.

A bird couple resting happily in the warmth of their nest on a nearby tree saw all this. They felt pity on the ignorant monkeys. The male bird said to the leader of the group, "Sir! the glow warms does not kindle fire. They glow only. Do not waste your time, find another way for litting the fire".

This the monkey leader took as a great insult and grew angry over the small bird. He ordered his group of monkeys

"Kill the birds and destroy their nests. These birds do not know how to respect wise and great like us". Soon the monkeys caught the birds and wrang their necks till death.

THE PET MONGOOSE

Once upon a time there lived a farmer along with his wife in a small house on the out skirts of a tiny village. Both husband and wife worked in the fields all the day long for their living. One day they found a badly wounded mongoose near their house in a deplorable condition.

The farmer and his wife felt pity. They cared and nursed till the mongoose became normal. From the one words the mongoose became their favourite pet. In due course of time a son was born to them. When the child grew he started playing with mongoose. Mongoose liked the child and took care of him.

One day both farmer and wife had to go to the fields leaving the child to the care of mongoose. They went out with reluctant heart to work in the fields.

While the mongoose was moving here and there a big poisonous, snake crawled into the house. Slowly it moved towards the child. The snake was about to bite the child then the mongoose saw the snake and attacked it. There was a severe fight between the snake and the mongoose. Mongoose fought bravely and killed the snake. Thus the brave mongoose saved the child.

In the evening while the farmer and his wife were returning from the fields, the mongoose went out to greet them. The farmer saw the blood smeared mouth of the mongoose. He got angry. He did not think properly for a while even. He decided that mongoose had killed his child. In an impulse he killed the mongoose with an axe that was in his hands.

When they entered into the house, they saw the child playing joyfully. Around the child they saw a dead snake cut into pieces. The farmer realised his mistake and repented for the same.

❑❑❑